RUNNING A SUCCESSFUL LIBRARY CARD CAMPAIGN

A How-To-Do-It Manual for Librarians

Patrick Jones

HOW-TO-DO-IT MANUALS FOR LIBRARIANS

NUMBER 119

NEAL-SCHUMAN PUBLISHERS, INC.
New York, London

Published by Neal-Schuman Publishers, Inc.
100 Varick Street
New York, NY 10013

Printed and bound in the United States of America.

ISBN 1-55570-438-7

DEDICATION

To Houston, Texas, Mayor Lee B. Brown for his vision of getting every child a library card.

CONTENTS

LIST OF FIGURES

FOREWORD

Is there anything more American than a library card? More magical? More empowering?

A library card is more than an ID. It's a symbol of what the library offers and what it represents in our democracy. From cradle to grave, a library card signifies the opportunity for learning and enjoyment.

What could be an easier sell?

The fact is that with growing numbers of kids turning to the Internet instead of libraries, it's more important than ever that we reach out to children and their families, not just with a card but with reasons to use it.

It was Secretary of Education William J. Bennett who inspired an intensified sign-up effort when he said back in 1986, " . . . every child should have a library card and use it." Leaders of the American Library Association (ALA) and the National Commission on Libraries and Information Science (NCLIS) took Bennett's remark as a challenge. The first National Library Card Sign-Up Month was observed in September 1987. As director of the ALA's Public Information Office, I helped to create posters, promotional strategies, ads, and tip sheets to support libraries in strengthening their library card outreach. It would be less than honest to say this effort was met with overwhelming enthusiasm. In fact, I distinctly remember some librarians scoffing, "We do that already."

But that was then. Since then, many more libraries have gotten hip to the power of a library card to market their services. *Running a Successful Library Card Campaign: A How-To-Do-It Manual* is their story. It's a story that is easily replicated in almost any community. Whether it's a grocery store providing free milk and cookies for classes with 100 percent sign-up or visiting nurses distributing library card kits to parents of newborns, you're bound to find an idea or two or 20 with a price tag you can afford.

The author, Patrick Jones, helped to mastermind the Houston Public Library's Power Card Campaign, one of the most ambitious and successful sign-up efforts to date. In its first two years, the campaign registered more than 200,000 children for library cards. Juvenile circulation jumped more than 20 percent. The campaign also generated a significant budget increase for the library, a fresh new image, heightened visibility throughout the community, and gained powerful new allies among businesses, government, media, and schools.

Running a Successful Library Card Campaign begins with Jones's insider account of the Houston campaign, how it worked, its strengths, and shortcomings. But it doesn't stop there. Jones profiles successful campaigns of more than a dozen libraries in urban, suburban, and rural areas around the country. These libraries have generously shared their best practices and lessons learned that extended, in some cases, to redesign of the card itself and amending key policies.

You'll also find "What Works and Why," an A-Z summary of how to plan and implement a library card campaign, including ideas for seeking additional resources. I particularly like the emphasis on staff involvement at all levels and the added value of a library card campaign in building staff pride and morale.

Running a Successful Library Card Campaign is more than a how-to-do-it manual. Crammed with creative, fun, and doable ideas, it also provides the inspiration and rationale to do them. In the Gallery of Successful Library Card Campaign Programs, you'll find examples of library campaign materials, including place mats, posters, library card applications, letters to parents and teachers, tally sheets, and report forms. It's hard to imagine anyone reading this book and not saying at least once, *"I can do that!"*

On a personal level, an added pleasure is that I remember Patrick Jones from his days as a page at the Genesee District Library in Flint, Michigan. Patrick is a library success story if ever there was one. But, as this book demonstrates, he is far from alone in his passion for reaching out to kids. The creativity and dedication with which libraries and their staffs approach this task is awesome.

Promoting library card sign-up makes good sense on many levels. First and foremost, it directly supports the library's mission of making knowledge and information freely and widely available. The fact that it makes libraries look good is a secondary but no less valuable incentive. No library can ever have too much goodwill, especially when it translates into financial, political, and other support.

The vision of every child having a library card and using it is just that—a vision. It's one that we must continually strive to attain. I encourage you to read this book, learn, enjoy, and keep the vision alive.

Linda Wallace
Partner, Library Communication Strategies
Chicago, Illinois
Director, ALA Public Information Office, 1985-2000

PREFACE

Do you remember the excitement of receiving your first library card? You can see the excitement on the faces of young children showing off their cards to parents and librarians. It is their first "pass" to explore everything that libraries contain, sample everything libraries do. That first card can change a child into a lifelong patron.

A library card is so very basic that librarians overlook the power it represents. We disregard the design—even though it presents one of our best marketing opportunities. In our monthly reports and annual documents, we report lots of statistics. Yet we often fail to ascertain the number of people holding cards or the amount of budget we spend trying to get people to get and to use them. Instead, we take for granted that people have them, but perhaps our biggest mistake is taking for granted that all people want to have a library card.

Librarians often assume everyone knows all about libraries, but they don't. At a dinner party or some other function where you find yourself surrounded by non-librarians, the group will be amazed when you tell them stories about answering reference questions. Most of them had no idea that anyone can call or visit the library and that it is our job, indeed our pleasure, to find information for customers. Because it is what we do, we take it for granted. The similar assumption that "everyone has a library card" can be even more prevalent—even when statistics tell us otherwise. Many adults have not used a card in years.

It's time for our library community to gain a new vision of the mighty yet humble library card. Rather than being "old fashioned" and for school-use only, library cards are the key in many library systems to accessing the latest technology of the computer revolution. As libraries strive to become increasingly relevant to users, a library card is fast becoming a modern passport to privilege.

Running a Successful Library Card Campaign: A How-To-Do-It Manual addresses the compelling need to enroll as many users as possible. As libraries move more and more to online databases and e-books, library card campaigns will become increasingly important. Not only so that people can use these wonderful products, but also so that librarians can control, manage, count, and evaluate their use. Lots of library systems have revamped their cards, but few have taken the opportunity to also revamp their image through a library card campaign. Have you ever heard this classic advertising rallying cry: "You don't sell the steak, you sell the sizzle"? Think of the steak as all the traditional things people know libraries offer. The sizzle is all the new stuff that most of our customers don't and often can't believe we offer to them for free. People need to hear the sizzle as they slide their library card out of their wallet.

Running a Successful Library Card Campaign: A How-To-Do-It Manual uses the exemplary library card campaigns of various public libraries. It shows you how to plan, promote, and implement your own campaign. Library card campaigns can be year-long events or small projects done during September to celebrate the American Library Association's National Library Card Sign-Up Month. Large urban libraries with multiple branches serving can undertake massive campaigns millions of people. Library systems serving a much smaller number use their ingenuity to achieve similar goals. Most campaigns are undertaken, correctly, in partnerships with schools and most are focused, in some part, on signing on children.

My personal experience is an ongoing inspiration. I had just started working as the manager of youth programs for the Houston Public Library when I learned that Mayor Lee B. Brown had pledged to put a library card in the hands of every school age child. I was involved in the planning, development, implementation, and evaluation of the campaign, from soon after its inception through the time I left the Houston Public Library two years later. When the Mayor first proposed that every child get a library card, just over 100,000 children and teens held library cards from the Houston Public Library. By the time the Power Card Challenge had wrapped up its three year mission "to boldly go where no library card campaign had gone before," the number of Houston children and teens packing the power of library card stood just under 303,000. It was the most exciting, frustrating, and ultimately rewarding professional experience in my over twenty years of working in public libraries.

Certainly one of the objectives of the Power Card Challenge was to increase the awareness of the Houston Public Library throughout the community. Through the media campaign, the Power Card became the Library's identity, and in doing so also gave the organization a focus, a renewed energy, and a new high profile, not just in the city of Houston but nationally as well. Even now when I speak at conferences and mention that I worked in Houston, people ask about the Power Card.

That campaign was about trying to reach children and teens the library had been missing. Circulation of juvenile materials at the Houston Public Library increased over 33 percent in the period of the Power Card—demonstrating that children and teens were putting their new cards to use. In some branch libraries, in particular those in neighborhoods with a high number of children classed "at-risk," those numbers were even higher. It wasn't just a matter of promoting the need for all children to get library cards, but also to educating many segments of the public as to exactly what public libraries do and what a card could mean for their child.

We tried everything and learned many valuable lessons. Some of it worked, some of it didn't. There was a tremendous diversity of response to the program. I don't want to pretend that every person who worked for the Houston Public Library embraced the campaign because that just isn't true, nor did every child get a library card. Most will agree, though, that the campaign changed people. The enthusiasm was infectious.

Running a Successful Library Card Campaign: A How-To-Do-It Manual also explores the disconnection from near-ubiquitous library use with children to the drastic decline with adults. While some library systems can boast over 50 percent of their population signed up for cards, many report much smaller numbers. How can a successful library card campaign program win back lost patrons and sign up new recruits?

The first two chapters of this book investigate common themes before venturing into an examination of individual programs. Chapter 1, "FAQ: First Ask Questions" is a handy overview. Chapter 2 looks at the origins of the national effort by the American Library Association to create National Library Card Sign-Up Month in September.

The succeeding chapters examine special campaigns that all reaped great results. In Chapter 3, we'll focus on the Power Card Challenge in Houston. This campaign was spurred on by the mayor's announced goal to get every child in the city a library card and to get them to use it. Houston is certainly not the only large urban library that has undertaken such an ambitious library card campaign. *Running a Successful Library Card Campaign* examines nine other major urban areas in-depth. There are also imaginative, innovative, and successful programs from medium and small library systems with just a few branches. There are even one-room city or rural libraries that, lacking the resources of the larger systems, have still managed successful campaigns to sign up more users. The next to last chapter looks at a recent state-wide library card campaign from South Carolina that involved the State Library and the state association of school librarians.

The final chapter, "What Works and Why," examines the common themes from the various library card campaigns to find out what lessons librarians learned, what mistakes they made, and what libraries interested in replicating these projects need to know. By presenting an alphabet of best practices, libraries can learn some of the pitfalls to avoid and some of the leaps to make. In addition to looking at the practice of library card campaigns, this chapter will also integrate the science of organizational psychology. Most library card campaigns are projects that require or often cause changes in how a library does business. By drawing on the rich literature from organizational psychology, we can better learn and understand the elements of success.

Following the best practices is an extensive gallery sampling many of the campaigns highlighted in this book. These terrific graphics display flyers, posters, letters, and other documents that demonstrate the unique approach of individual campaigns. Please remember that these documents should inspire your creative juices, *not* wear out the toner in your copy machine. They are examples and should not be duplicated without the written consent of the library that created them. For links to Web pages related to library card campaigns, please visit my Web site at: www. connectingya.com

This is a how-to-do-it manual. We look at specific, good examples from a wide range of libraries for the best practices in marketing and managing. If libraries are going to change other's lives, then we need to begin by making sure young people use them. First they need a library card. To do that, they need someone to see they get one: someone like you.

ACKNOWLEDGMENTS

I would like to thank Library Director Barbara Gubbin and the staff, especially the youth services librarians, of the Houston Public Library for making the Power Card such a powerful success. In particular, thanks to the Power Card Steering Committee: Brenda Tirrell, Alison Landers, Andrea Lapsley, Janine Golden, Sheryl Berger, Fred Schumacher, and Gail Hicks. Also, thanks to Robert Gibbs and Cathy Guy of Reliant Energy for sharing and supporting the Mayor's vision. Finally, thanks to the school librarians with the Houston Independent School District and all the other school districts who answered the Power Card Challenge.

I would like to acknowledge the following for their contribution to this work by supplying documents and other information about library card campaigns:

American Library Association Library (IL):
    Karen Muller
Austin Public Library (TX):
    Ann Minner, Nancy Toombs, and Anne Morris
Bellevue Public Library (OH):
    JoEllen Boos
Berlin-Peck Memorial Library (CT):
    Cathy Nelson
Birmingham Public Library (AL):
    Pat Ryan
Carroll County Public Library (MD):
    Marcia Schaffe
Central Rappahannock Regional Library (VA):
    Rebecca Purdy
Charlton Public Library (GA):
    Dorinda Montgomery
Chicago Public Library (IL):
    Cindy Welch and Elizabeth Huntoon
Clayton County Public Library (GA):
    Janice Arcuria
Columbus Metro Gahanna Branch (OH):
    Martha Lund
Contra Costa Public Library (CA):
    Annemarie Meyer
Des Moines Public Library (IA):
    Jan Danielson Kaiser
Dickson County Public Library (TN):
    Suzanne Robinson

Durham County Library (NC):
  Pam Jaskot
Eccles-Lesher Memorial Library (PA):
  Nancy Shanafelt
Evanston Public Library (IL):
  Sharon Aguagenti
Fountaindale Public Library District (IL):
  Carol Feldberg
Jacksboro Public Library (TN):
  Peg Southerland
Jefferson County Public Library (CO):
  Kay Pride
Jervis Public Library (NY):
  Lisa Matte
Jessamine County Public Library (KY):
  Colleen Hall
Long Beach Public Library (CA):
  Lynda Poling and Christine Burcham
Los Angeles Public Library (CA):
  Peter V. Persic
Lumpkin County Library (GA):
  Lori Wilkins
Missoula Public Library (MT):
  Bette Ammon, Kathy Mitchell, and Linette
  Ivanovitch
Mooresville Public Library (IN):
  Lynn Jurewicz
Multnomah County Public Library (OR):
  Ruth Allen, Sara Ryan, Ellen Fader, and Jackie
  Partch
Muscogee Public Library (GA):
  Silvia Bunn
New Orleans Public Library (LA):
  David Winkler-Schmit
Newport Public Library (CA):
  Judy Kelley
Niles Public Library (IL):
  Valerie Stern
Oshkosh Public Library (WI):
  Laurie Magee
Palmyra Bicentennial Public Library (MO):
  Carol Brentlinger
Pemberville Public Library (OH):
  Laurel Rakas

Perry County District Library (OH):
>Robin L. Gibson
Philadelphia Free Library (PA):
>Mary Flournoy and Sandy Farrell
Phoenix Public Library (AZ):
>Kim van der Veen
Pikes Peak District Library (CO):
>Nancy Milvid
Putnam County Library (OH):
>Traci Moritz
Rabun Public Library (MO):
>Julia Williams
Rancho Cucamonga Public Library (CA):
>Renne Tobin
Randolph County Library (GA):
>Leigh Wiley
Rapid City Public Library (SD):
>Susan Hotalling
Richmond Memorial Library (NY):
>Sandy Gillard
San Jose Public Library (CA):
>Cornelia VanAken-Sanks
Satilla Public Library (GA):
>Rondalea Stark
Scottsbluff Public Library (NE):
>Deb Carlson
South Carolina State Library (SC):
>Jane G. Connor
Spokane Public Library (WA):
>Dolly Richendrfer
Sudbury Public Library (ON):
>Claire Zuliani
University of Illinois Archives (IL):
>Christopher Prom and Kate Meehan
Vigo County Public Library (IN):
>June Dunbar
Washington-Centerville Public Library (OH):
>Kayrene Elkins
Yukon Public Library (OH):
>Sara Schieman

On a personal note, I would like to thank the folks at the Hennepin County Library, in particular Mark Ranum and Gretchen Wronka, and Virginia Bush and Cathy Hoffman of the Minneapolis Public Library, for their help getting me settled in

Minnesota. Thanks to the usual suspects of Brent Chartier, Ken Rasak, Patricia Taylor, Tim Retzloff, and Betty Jones for their support. And to Erica for letting me try the also-Flint-Michigan-born-Christopher-Paul-Curtis-inspired "year off work" to write this book and complete other projects.

CREDITS

- A version of Chapter 3, "Packing the Power," originally appeared in *Public Libraries* (May/June 2000). Used with permission.
- Chapter 16, "What Works and Why," co-written with Erica Klein (doctoral student in industrial/organizational psychology at the University of Houston).
- Documents in the gallery of this book were reprinted with permission. **All documents retain copyright of the original creators and should not be reproduced without written consent.**
- Key art and slogan for the 1998 Los Angeles Public Library Card Campaign designed at the direction of Conlon Schwartz Advertising and Design. Used with permission.
- Power Card and Power Card Challenge are trademarked by Reliant Energy and are used with permission. Reliant Energy is the title sponsor of the Power Card Challenge.

1 FAQ: FIRST ASK QUESTIONS

The subtitle of this book is somewhat presumptuous. It is not so much a "how-to-do-it" manual outlining step-by-step instructions as it is a "how-it-was-done" manual reporting on success stories. The reason for this is simple: there is no one best way to undertake a library card campaign because the details of such a project are determined by the goals. And the goals for every organization will be different based not only on desired outcomes, but also on the capacity of organizations. Often, people look to manuals such as these for ideas, and there are within these pages hundreds of them from library systems of all sizes, but it seems the purpose of professional development reading is even more often about finding answers. The answer of how to do a library card campaign thus depends on the questions.

Library cards are nothing new. They are a "product" that libraries have been offering their public for years, so why do a campaign? That simple question needs a good answer before any library should consider, unless under a directive from a funder, undertaking any sort of library card campaign of any scale. But that is only the first of several *big* questions that must be first asked and answered. As you read this manual, you will learn how many systems—from those as large as Los Angeles Public to those so small that the director is the entire staff—answered basic questions. Before you read on and certainly before you undertake a library card campaign, you need to ask the following questions. The questions will determine the answers you find useful in this book. The ideas will come not only by duplicating best practices, but also by viewing a library card campaign as a process of creative problem solving.

WHO IS THE AUDIENCE?

√ Is the audience every person in the library's service area or just a target audience?
√ Can the audience be made larger by changing policies or regulations, which would allow more people to be eligible for cards?
√ What is the value in selecting only one target audience?

√ If only a target audience, then which one? Adults? Children? School-age children? New immigrants?

√ What do members of the target audience have in common? What are the differences?

√ What are the current barriers to members of this target audience obtaining library cards?

√ Within this larger target audience can it be divided into market segments?

√ Within the target audience are certain market segments easier to reach? Others harder to reach?

WHY ARE PEOPLE NOT GETTING CARDS?

√ What, if any, barriers exist to current residents obtaining library cards?

√ Which of these barriers are internal to the library (for example, which barriers are related to library procedures, policies, or regulations)?

√ Which of these barriers are external to the library (for example, which barriers are related to demographics, transportation, or other factors)?

√ How can the library overcome such barriers by developing new strategies or working with community partners?

√ What have been the strong and weak points of previous library card campaigns or large-scale projects?

√ What has the library learned in such projects that can be translated to a library card campaign?

√ What issues related to staffing present a barrier?

√ What issues related to resources, in particular financial resources, present a barrier?

√ What bridges must be built to overcome these barriers?

√ What does the library know about the public it has not reached?

WHO IS THE STAFF INVOLVED?

√ What staff is involved in planning the library card campaign?

√ What contingency does each member of the planning team represent and are all-important players represented?

√ What primary staff will be involved in carrying out the campaign?

√ What training will staff need to undertake such a campaign?

√ What resources or tools will staff need?

√ What parts of each person's job can be eliminated to take on the new work from the campaign?

√ Will more staff need to be hired?

√ At what level (for example, librarian, shelvers, clerk) is staffing most needed to carry out the campaign?

√ How can volunteers be utilized to help staff with the campaign?

√ What incentives will motivate staff to work toward the goals of the campaign?

√ What changes in scheduling might be required to allow staff to implement the campaign?

WHO IN THE COMMUNITY CAN HELP WITH THE EFFORT?

√ What roles will public schools play in the campaign?

√ What roles can private, parochial, alternative, charter, or home schools play?

√ What roles can the early childhood community play?

√ Is there one corporate or business sponsor to take the lead?

√ What businesses have a vested interest in an educated work force?

√ What businesses have a history of working with the library or with educational institutions?

√ What can the library offer potential partners?

√ What roles can neighborhood associations, community groups, and other locally based organizations play?

√ What role can city or county departments, such as parks, play in the campaign?

√ What role can colleges, universities, and community colleges play in the campaign?

HOW CAN PEOPLE SIGN UP FOR CARDS?

√ Do library card sign-ups have to take place in the library?
√ Can library card sign-ups take place in the community?
√ Can library card sign-ups take place in schools?
√ Can library card sign-ups take place over the Internet?
√ What policies limit library card sign-ups?
√ What purpose do these limits serve and are they consistent with a library card sign-up effort?
√ Can policies that limit sign-ups or reregistration be amended, suspended, or eliminated?

WHAT ARE THE MEASURABLE GOALS?

√ What metrics will measure success of the campaign?
√ Are you looking to increase the total number of library cardholders?
√ Are you looking to increase the number of certain types of library cardholders?
√ Are you looking to increase the number of persons who reregister for a library card?
√ Are you looking only to measure the number of new library cardholders?
√ Are you looking to measure use of cards to check out books?
√ Are you looking to measure use of cards to check out any materials or use any library service?
√ Are you looking to increase the total number of cards in use?
√ Are you looking to increase program attendance or summer reading participation?
√ Are you looking for increased door counts, reference transactions, or other measures?
√ Are you looking to increase all measures by a net total or to increase per capita use?

WHAT ARE THE COLLATERAL GOALS OR OUTCOMES FOR THE LIBRARY?

√ Other than increases in use or library card registration, what other outcomes are important for the library?

√ Can you measure the amount of positive public relations?

√ Can you measure the increase/decrease in staff morale?

√ Can you measure the increase/decrease in the public's knowledge of the library?

√ Can you measure the increase/decrease in the overall visibility of the library in the community?

WHEN AND WHERE WILL THE CAMPAIGN OCCUR?

√ When is the best time to undertake such a campaign?

√ Can the campaign tie in with national initiatives, such as National Library Card Sign-Up Month or National Library Week?

√ How long should the campaign last?

√ Should the campaign be designed as a "one-shot" campaign or designed to be duplicated every year?

√ Should different audiences be approached at different times of the year?

√ Where in the community can the library find potential customers for library cards?

√ Where in the community can the library find underserved populations?

These are certainly not the only questions that any library thinking about undertaking a library card campaign should consider. Plans for a large-scale campaign involve hundreds of big questions and thousands of small ones. All aspects of managing library resources, from staffing to budgeting to organization development, play a part in putting together a successful library card campaign. What follows are success stories of library systems, large and small, that have each, based on the needs of their communities and their organizations, developed innovative answers to these questions. If a reference question is a matter of simple problem solving, then a library card campaign is also problem solving, if at a larger scale. It seems that the libraries that found answers that are not pat and not tied to the past, and that focused more on the customer than on the library solved their problem of increasing library card registration.

2 GETTING CARDED: THE AMERICAN LIBRARY ASSOCIATION'S NATIONAL LIBRARY CARD SIGN-UP MONTH CAMPAIGN

"By the end of the 1986–87 school year, every child should obtain a library card—and use it," wrote Secretary of Education William Bennett in *What Works* (Bennett, 1987:7). He went on to suggest that it would take a national campaign to achieve this goal. By 1987 the American Library Association (ALA) and the National Commission on Libraries and Information Science (NCLIS) had put together such a campaign. The campaign, aimed more at parents than at children, was build around the theme "The Best Gift You'll Ever Give Your Child—A Library Card." A grant from the Reader's Digest Foundation of $85,000 provided funding for ALA to mail a library card sign-up tip kit to every school and public library in September. The funding also paid for radio, TV, and print public service announcements in English and Spanish.

The official kickoff for the campaign was held October 14, 1987, on the National Mall. Pizza Hut, sponsors of the national Book It! reading incentive program, underwrote the kickoff event, complete with music, food, and entertainment. Secretary Bennett, along with ALA President Margaret Chisholm, NCLIS chair Jerald Newman and vice chair Bessie Moore, and congressman/librarian Major Owens, attended the ceremony, which also included more than 500 school children from the metro area. Also present were a group of very special guests: 224 children from Norrisville Elementary School in Maryland. This was the first school, on record as part of the campaign, to have a public library card issued to every student in the school.

The drive at Norrisville Elementary began, as hundreds of other library card campaigns would in the coming years, with a phone call. Frances V. Sedney, the children's coordinator for the Harford County Library System, picked up the telephone and called Mary

Ellen Kennedy, the supervisor of library services in the Harford County Schools. Together, but with the support of other library staff and school personnel, they launched a series of events that resulted in every child in the school getting a card. The final event took place on a September day when the children walked single file from their school to their local branch of the Harford County Library where each received a personalized library card. After receiving their cards, the children assembled in front of their school, proudly holding up their cards, for a group photo. One third grader at the school noted "after all the other kids in all the other schools find out that we could do it—then they'll want to do it. I feel good about it because parents will think about it now and maybe get cards for the whole family" ("National Library Card Campaign Kicked Off on D.C. Mall," 1987:13).

While October 14, 1987, marked the official launch of the program, many libraries were ahead of the game. In West Virginia, Frederick J. Glazer, the state library commission director, and Tom McNeel, the state school superintendent, cosponsored the "Library Cards for Fun and Profit" campaign. All schools that achieved 100 percent sign-up rates for their students for public library cards were eligible for a grand prize of $500 in books and other library materials. The county with the highest percentage of library cardholders won $1,000 worth of prizes. At the ceremony, NCLIS chair Newman was able to announce that 174 schools and three counties in West Virginia, which totaled over 50,000 students, were fully registered for cards. In some libraries, the demand for registration was so great that libraries ran out of registration forms and were enrolling students on the back of recycled catalog cards.

In Missouri, a statewide effort was launched under the banner of "For Every Child in Missouri: A Library Card." The state library mailed large quantities of promotional materials to public libraries in the state to use in conjunction with their local campaigns. One promotional piece was a bright yellow postcard for children to record their name, library, and favorite book. The postcards were addressed to the state librarian, Monteria Hightower, and gathered by libraries for return to the state library. Every child who signed one of the postcards and had a library card got a bright sticker with a heart on it proclaiming, "I use my Missouri Library Card."

In New York, the state library made funds available for grants to library systems for projects that would encourage family reading and library registration of new families and children as part of the "best gift" campaign. Even without the grant, many libraries were already looking at methods to increase library card registration. In some cases, this effort meant designing public relations campaigns or cooperating with schools. In some instances, however, the desire to get children a library card led libraries to reexamine their policies and procedures. Several systems identified barriers within their registration process that kept kids from getting cards and they set about to remove these barriers.

After the success of the first year, ALA set about to make the national library card campaign something other than a one-time event. Following a joint resolution from Congress in 1988 proclaiming September to be National Library Card Sign-Up Month, a huge promotional campaign directed from the ALA Public Information Office began focusing on students in elementary through high school for the start of the 1988–1989 school year. Tying library card campaigns to the reopening of school served to reinforce the message that library cards, like pencils and pens, are an essential school supply. ALA sent out press releases, placed articles, and designed public service announcements to appear in a wide variety of publications aimed at youth or parents.

Chicago-based corporations McDonald's and Sears both joined the 1988 campaign as national sponsors. Sears included public service messages in its back-to-school catalog. The catalog also featured fashion layouts in the boys' section that were set in a library. McDonald's distributed as part of its Happy Meals a message promoting library card sign-up. The Happy Meal boxes featured a punch-out library card which kids could take to their local library to get a real card. The instructions on the box reminded children to take an adult or parent with them to complete the application. With nearly all McDonald's restaurants participating, the message was delivered in millions of Happy Meals sold during the fall of 1988.

The huge advertising agency, J. Walter Thompson USA, came on board to do pro bono work for ALA. They helped develop a new series of promotional materials for the library card campaign, including banners, bookmarks, and a campaign tip sheet. Emerging from this campaign as well was a special poster featuring Keshia Knight Pulliam of the popular TV show *The Cosby Show*. Keshia, who played Cosby's youngest child on the show, was shown in the poster holding up a library card. The slogan at the bottom said, "I got carded at the library."

In 1989 ALA created a contest to reward the best library card campaign. The first contest was won by the Hector Public Library, a small library in Minnesota. Jill Sing, head librarian for the winning library noted, "We placed articles in the local newspaper, put up posters everywhere, visited classrooms, placed notices in church bulletins, sports bulletins, and 4H newsletters."

The effort resulted in a 71 percent increase in sign-ups and earned the library a $1,000 gift certificate donated by World Book. The 311 new cards issued in Hector were part of a total of over 21,000 new library cards issued in September 1989.

Throughout the 1990s ALA continued support for National Library Card Sign-Up Month and the contest for best campaign. ALA also continued to produce special materials for libraries to use during their own campaigns, such as the "Get a Life—Get A Library Card" T-shirt and a poster featuring characters from the Disney animated film *Beauty and the Beast*. The Disney tie-in demonstrates ALA's work with the entertainment industry to produce graphics and develop sponsorships to support projects like National Library Card Sign-Up Month. From the 1996 materials featuring the actors from the film *Matilda* (based on the children's book by Roald Dahl) to the 1997 materials featuring Lassie up to the 2000 materials featuring Marc Brown's Arthur, ALA continues to promote library card sign-ups by using popular characters to remind children and parents to get a library card.

While every year the materials were slightly different, by "creating" National Library Card Sign-Up Month, the ALA Public Information Office provided the basic tools, including press releases and media announcements, to any library wanting to undertake a library card campaign. The lessons of the very first campaign, however, would prove useful: work closely with schools, offer incentives for participation, and above all, celebrate success. While the first campaign focused on motivating parents to sign up their children for library cards, the artwork of many subsequent campaigns has been aimed directly at youth. Armed with the READ posters produced by ALA Graphics and the materials produced by ALA's Public Information Office, the library's leading professional organization has played a principal role in promoting that every child get a library card.

REFERENCES

Bennett, William, 1986. *What Works*. Washington, D.C.: U.S. Department of Education.

"National Library Card Campaign Kicked Off on D.C. Mall." 1987. *School Library Journal* 34(December):13–15.

3 PACKING THE POWER: HOUSTON PUBLIC LIBRARY'S POWER CARD CHALLENGE

Books were the first rungs on the ladder I, like many others, used to climb out of poverty. Now, it's my goal to see that every school age child in Houston gets a library card.—Lee B. Brown

At his inauguration on January 2, 1998, the new mayor of Houston, Texas, Mayor Lee B. Brown, proposed that grand vision. Within a week of that announcement, the Houston Public Library (HPL) pulled together a committee to begin planning to turn the mayor's vision into a reality. Such a huge project was unprecedented in the history of the library, or for that matter, most urban public libraries. A review of the professional literature netted little information about successful models for a library the size of HPL. Serving the fourth largest city in the United States, the library has a Central Library/administrative complex, 35 branch libraries, and three other service points.

A small work team was put together by new Assistant Director Alison Landers. Landers had joined the library as the assistant director for public services just one week before the mayor's announcement. Landers gathered the managers of the technical services, public information, and marketing departments as well as representative children's librarians, desk staff, and public service managers from across the library system to develop a plan. Working quickly, the team presented the mayor with an ambitious strategy, which included the need for more staff, more materials, more equipment, more printing, and therefore a lot more money. The mayor backed up his bold words with a bolder action: a 13 percent increase in HPL's operating budget, with the majority of funding directed toward the library card sign-up program.

The funding would go toward purchasing more materials for children and teens so they would have something to check out with those cards. Funding also went toward fixtures and furnishings to display these new materials, for staff to work circulation desks to check out the materials and to handle increased registration activity, and "Power Card librarians" who would work directly in the community promoting the library program. These librarians, based out of the library's six administrative regions, would provide support for the campaign by doing outreach directly or by being "on the desk" while the branch staff ventured out into the community. The library also created a position of Power Card project manager to oversee the day-to-day workings on the campaign. Money was also budgeted for new library cards themselves. The timing of the mayor's announcement was fortunate as the library was about to change automation vendors and every patron would need to get a new library card. Funding was put aside for these new cards, which would emerge, however, as much different from the flimsy, brown-and-white paper document which had been serving as the library card.

This 13 percent budget increase was one of the largest in the history of the library. Like many libraries in Texas, HPL had fallen on hard times in the middle 1980s and year by year was recouping its loss of budget. This dramatic increase thus represented not only a desire for the mayor to see his program enacted, but served additionally as a vote of confidence for the direction of the library. The previous year the library had aimed to increase youth library cardholders with a campaign to register every third grader in the Houston Independent School District (HISD) for a library card. That program worked very well at some schools, not so well at others. Third grade was the target audience, as one of Governor George W. Bush's prime educational initiatives was to ensure that all students were reading up to grade level by third grade.

The third grade "Cards for Kids" program was not designed to be a pilot program. Although at the time it was not designed to be a pilot program, having that experience gave the public library staff some insight about what did and didn't work. In particular, even though high-level communication was established with the school district, some schools didn't participate—and many that did seemed to do so without enthusiasm, despite the incentives offered to schools with the most sign-ups. To generate more sign-ups, more excitement would need to be generated, not just among teachers and school librarians, but also among parents, the general public, and the library staff itself.

The mayor's vision, however, was for all school-age children to get library cards, not just third graders. The potential target market just in HISD was 225,000 students. But not every student who lives in Houston attends HISD schools; many of the suburban school districts consist of schools both inside and outside the city limits. Like many city library systems, the library required nonresidents to pay a fee ($40). The geography and political outlines of Houston certainly didn't help as several independent cities in the Houston metro had their own libraries and the unincorporated areas that were served by the large county library system created a huge body of nonresidents who drove, worked, or lived near branches of the Houston Public Library. This fee presented a substantial barrier to the success of the program. For example, students who lived in independent cities, such as Bellaire or West University, would be ineligible for cards although they attended school inside the city of Houston. Further, Houston has a large private school community. Attendees of most of the private schools consist of a mix of city residents and nonresidents. Thus, private school principals and superintendents of suburban school districts were concerned about the ability of the program to reach their students if only half of the students would be entitled to free cards, while the other half who were not city residents would need to pay a fee. The superintendent of one of the largest suburban school districts, which had three Houston Public Library branches near schools but also branches of the county library system, told the HPL that his district would not be interested in participating until all students could get free cards.

Working with the Houston City Council, Library Director Barbara Gubbin had the nonresident fee waived for children under the age of 19, thus removing the largest obstacle to the success of the program. That move proved so successful and popular that, for the second year of the program, the waiver was extended to include adults, thereby allowing teachers, parents, and caregivers to check out materials. The waiver covered not just children and adults within Harris County, where most of the city of Houston lies, but also in the 11 contiguous counties. The challenge became even greater as the target market boomed to almost 500,000 from adding in students in the major suburban school districts as well as 120,000 students in private schools. To sign up every school-age child for a library card would be a powerful challenge that couldn't be met in just one year. Instead, the library decided to attempt to reach this goal over a three-year period beginning in July 1, 1998, and ending on June 30, 2001.

WHAT WAS THE POWER CARD CHALLENGE?

At a town hall meeting soon after announcing his library card campaign, Mayor Brown was asked about library services. During his response to the question, he remarked how a library card would empower young people and reminded the audience that the notion "knowledge is power" would become even more important in the 21st century. Soon after, the library's director of marketing, Andrea Lapsley, approached the institution in the city of Houston that knew the most about power: Houston Industries, the parent company to Houston Lighting and Power and Entex (now Reliant Energy). Reliant's director of community affairs, Robert Gibbs, was very interested in the mayor's program, and pledged the support of Reliant Energy. While the support was institutional in nature, it also stemmed from Mr. Gibbs's personal belief in the importance of public libraries (based on his childhood experience of taking part in his hometown library's summer reading program). Gibbs soon enlisted the support of members of his staff and others from Reliant to assist HPL in developing a program to meet the mayor's goal.

While the assistance was in part financial, just as important was Reliant's expertise. The library and Reliant decided early in the planning process that a simple library card campaign could not achieve the mayor's goal. Instead, the library and Reliant would need to develop a marketing plan to create, promote, and market the library card as if it were a new product. With a desire to appeal to young people and to focus on the empowering nature of library use, the library card was transformed into the "Power Card." The Power Card would be the "product" and "brand name" of the library. Reliant created a logo (the Power Critter), a color scheme (bright colors, with orange being the most prevalent), and a graphic design (a swirl of colors giving the appearance of energy). The card would be plastic, like a credit card, and feature the library's Web address as well as Reliant's logo. The design of the card itself was unique; it looked like few other library cards.

Reliant also helped prepare and pay for bilingual Power Card applications, bright colorful posters, and even brighter orange T-shirts (bearing the slogan "Pack the Power" and featuring the Reliant logo on the sleeve). Coupled with slogans such as "Small enough to fit into your wallet, big enough to change your life," the new library card and the sign-up campaign was off to a colorful and powerful start. Reliant gave the program a huge boost by including information about the Power Card program in their monthly utility bills, which reached over one million customers. Like many large corporations, Reliant had a program with local schools called "Education Ambassadors." The ambassadors soon found they had another powerful message to take to school: get a Power Card. Yet, perhaps most important, having Reliant Energy as the primary sponsor gave the library card campaign instant credibility in the community.

WHAT WERE THE GOALS OF THE POWER CARD CHALLENGE?

Since it provides free access to a wealth of resources, in particular for school age children needing materials for formal educational support, it seems obvious that every parent would want his or her child to have a library card. Yet only 100,000 Houston kids held library cards in January 1998. The campaign in the fall of 1997 to sign up third graders had increased that number, but less than a third of the students offered cards in that drive actually applied for and received the card. From experience, the library knew that despite its very best efforts, not every child, for a variety of cultural, economic, and other reasons, would receive parental permission (a parent signature is required by city ordinance) to get a card. The library knew it could not meet the goal to get every child a library card.

Instead, the library set three challenging yet obtainable goals for the initial year of the Power Card Challenge. The first goal was to see that every school-age child in public and private school was given an application for the Power Card and therefore provided with the opportunity to receive a card. Second, after looking at the success (and drawbacks) of its previous campaign, the library set a goal of obtaining 100,000 new cardholders. Reaching this goal would double the number of users but required only a 20 percent completion rate for the distributed applications. Increasing the number of cardholders, however, was merely part of the mayor's vision. In his inauguration speech he went on to say that every child should use his or her card. This created a third goal for the Power Card Challenge—to increase circulation of juvenile materials by 20 percent.

One of the first steps to meet these goals was creating a series of materials to introduce the program. The library created a Power Card application bearing the logo, the "Pack the Power" slogan, and the tag line "Get your own Power Card and you'll discover everything from the ABC's to the SAT's." These colorful applications were in English on one side, in Spanish on the other. They contained space for all the necessary information, plus a parent signature. Each application also bore the logo of Reliant Energy.

Just as important, each application contained a space for the parent to put a driver's license or ID number. Previous to the Power Card, any child wanting a library card would need to come into the library with a parent who could show a staff member a piece of identification. Under the Power Card program, the library merely requested that the information be provided on the application, but the parent need not present the information in person. As the campaign moved along, this requirement proved to be one of the key sticking points to getting applications returned, in particular from schools that did distribute and collect applications. It also become problematic at outreach events where often parents did not have or did not have on them the proper identification. The library decided that what was most important was getting a child a library card, not having a perfectly completed application. Those applications without ID would be processed, but with a note requesting that a parent supply the ID in person at a later time. Applications could not be processed, however, without a parent's signature or without complete information. While there were lots of decisions to be made along the way, this whole process was crucial, as well as symbolic. The message was simple: we want to get kids cards first and foremost, so let's knock down the barriers to making that happen. This wasn't a "victory" of public services over technical services, but rather a victory for the kids of Houston.

WHO ANSWERED THE POWER CARD CHALLENGE?

A program of such massive proportions would require more partners than Reliant Energy. The library first looked toward the schools. Working with the administration of HISD, the library arranged to have every student receive the bilingual Power Card application during the first week of school as part of each student's "opening day pack," which also contained other important forms for parents to sign. The Library did *not* require that teachers or school librarians collect applications, but asked that students and parents visit the library to get their cards. The library didn't want children to get cards just to get them or because a teacher made them, but rather because they wanted to get a card and/or because a parent wanted them to obtain their own library card. If the goal had been only to increase sign-ups, collecting applications at the schools might have been the plan. But since the goal was also to encourage use, the only way that could happen was if kids came into libraries.

The process of distributing applications to over 200 HISD schools was quite involved. The primary contact for HISD was not the head of school libraries (which was a vacant position during the summer when most of the Power Card final planning was going on), but rather a former principal, Sandra Satterwhite, who handled special projects for the superintendent and who also reported directly to the superintendent's chief of staff. Satterwhite delivered to the library a list of each HISD school, the number of expected students in the fall of 1998, and its "route number" for the school's delivery system. The library next set up an assembly line in the basement with the list, boxes and boxes of library card applications, and lots of brown envelopes. Summer workers, volunteers, and staff then began work preparing packets for each of the district's schools. On the front of each envelope was a bright green label stating "Power Card Applications." Inside was a cover letter from the superintendent of schools, Rod Paige, and instructions from the library about completing the applications.

The district's area administrators had been briefed during a meeting in early August 1999 and they then informed their principals that applications would be forthcoming. The library's head of delivery, Jacqui Nesbit, worked with the distribution personnel at HISD to arrange the transfer of items from the library to the school district's central distribution. From there, the applications went to schools where school staff and volunteers put them into opening day packets. School librarians also received a letter with instructions about the Power Card when they returned to school, as well as a phone call, fax, or e-mail from their local branch children's librarian about the Power Card. Whenever possible, the school librarian would be visited by a staff member from the public library to check out the supply of applications, as well as to drop off posters. And that was all just for one school district. There were 12 more school districts to be included in the campaign.

In September the six region managers of the library oversaw the distribution of Power Card applications in the other school districts in the Houston area. Houston is a huge, sprawling city, and a regional library like the Collier Regional Library served students going to HISD schools as well as those attending schools in the Spring Branch, North Forest, and Aldine school districts. The approach in each school system was unique. The region manager would work with the superintendent, or someone delegated by the superintendent, to work out the mechanics of dropping off applications and posters. For example, in the Alief School District, library staff attended a meeting of the district's school librarians to promote the program and distribute applications. For the Clear Creek School District, the program was more in the hands of the school principals who heard a speaker from a library during a back-to-school meeting and got a strong message from the school superintendent to participate in the program. Just as some schools were more enthusiastic about participating than others, so were some districts.

In October the library shifted its attention to the large private and parochial school community. In August every private and parochial school received a letter inviting their participation. Along with the letter was a postcard whereby schools could commit to supporting the Power Card Challenge and request applications for all of their students. Once the postcards were received, packets were put together for the participating schools. In October those packets were either mailed or sent through the interoffice delivery and then dropped off, along with posters, to the schools. Several private schools were also visited by library staff who set up sign-up tables in school libraries to collect the completed applications and hand out the new Power Cards. The library also worked with the manager of school libraries for the Catholic schools, and a representative attended meetings and promoted the Power Cards there.

In the following months other educational facilities and services (a charter school, home schoolers, Head Starts, juvenile detention facilities, alternative schools, and day care centers) and more suburban school districts were provided with applications. The staggering of the distribution of applications was deliberate. Even though more staff positions were created, it would be impossible to handle the expected deluge of work all during the month of September. The head of technical services for the library, Brenda Tirrell, closely worked with the desk supervisors at the regional buildings and at the Central Library to attempt to share the workload. Standards, such as all applications should be processed within a certain amount of time, were set and staff were urged to share work not just among the branches in their region, but also within the system. Thus, the Power Card very early on created opportunities for interlibrary cooperation that had been lacking the past. Staff at the Central Library, which had few schools in its service area, worked very hard helping out those branches that couldn't keep up with the application onslaught. Yet, many desk staff, despite the heavy workload, were enthusiastic about the program and loved to tell stories about young people racing into the library with their colorful Power Card applications filled out, ready, in many cases, to get their first library cards.

Although the mayor spoke of the need for every school-age child to get a card, the library wanted to make sure that all children got cards, even those who had not yet started school. With the wave of research about brain development, coupled with the library's training program that fall called "Babythink: Babies Belong in Libraries," a strong effort was made to reach the youngest of customers. Using a database obtained from the state agency charged with regulating day care centers, the library did a mass mailing in January to every licensed child care provider. Each center received a letter explaining the Power Card, a postcard so they could request applications, and a newly developed piece with a map of all the libraries on one side and "Frequently Asked Questions" about the Power Card on the other side. Hundreds of day care centers, some with fewer than 10 children and others with up to 100, requested and received applications.

But the bulk of the early action with the Power Card was taking place at schools. Many teachers, school librarians, principals, and administrators made a strong commitment to the Power Card Challenge, and in doing so they worked to reach 100 percent sign-up in their schools. One of the early successful programs was HISD's Key Middle School. The principal, working with her faculty, arranged a Power Card day where students brought completed applications to the school library and HPL staff was on hand to issue the cards. The Key Middle School program also became, in some ways, a model for future sign-up of every student at a particular school. In addition to getting their library cards, the students also heard a short presentation from the district's Chief of Staff Susan Sclafani. Although Sclafani was invited to the program by the school, having her in attendance was a real boost for the library. Even though she had spoken at the press conference announcing the Power Card, this was her first opportunity to see the library "in action" getting cards into the hands of HISD students. She, like the students, then enjoyed the library staff powering up enthusiasm among kids about using the library through booktalking, leading them in a Power Card chant, and the debut of children's librarian Nora Aaron's "Power Card Rap."

But as important as the program was in getting all students signed up for cards and "showing off" the program to the HISD administration, the first all-school sign-up had another side benefit. In order to staff such a program, librarians and desk staff throughout the entire region were brought together. While they all worked in the same geographical region, many were meeting their colleagues in other branches for the first time. The day ended with the library's public information officer, Sheryl Berger, taking a picture of the Key Middle School "crew." The photo documented for all of the staff involved in the outreach that they had been part of something very special, something that worked. Finally, the Key Middle School sign-up then became a "challenge" to other schools to see if they could achieve the same success.

Throughout the city, schools accommodated the library's outreach visit to promote the Power Card. Library staff made presentations and did sign-ups at parent nights during the fall, and in the winter and spring went into still more schools. On March 2, 1999, the library went all out with its Power Card promotion in celebration of Read Across America Day. Staff from every branch visited at least one school that day to promote the Power Card. In addition, at City Hall, the library joined with the heads of the reading and library departments for HISD to make a presentation before the Houston City Council to remind them that the Power Card program, by then all of seven months old, was still alive and well. Students (wearing red-and-white Dr. Seuss hats and bright orange Power Card T-shirts) from a downtown elementary school joined the HISD and HPL administration in the city council chambers. Later, another school, this time from a suburban school district that had achieved near 100 percent sign-up, would come to the city council to thank the council and the mayor for making the program possible.

Schools that achieved near 100 percent sign-ups were rewarded with a colorful banner funded by Reliant Energy, proclaiming "Our School Packs the Power." The presentation of these banners became huge events. Many of the events featured not just the principal of the school, but also members of the school board as well as a representative from the Houston City Council. In many cases, the library would provide entertainment, such as storytellers or magic shows. By the end of three years, nearly 100 schools had signed up at least 90 percent of their students to get Power Cards, with an equal distribution of HISD and other schools. Reliant Energy, the corporate sponsor of the Power Card Challenge, donated the bright two-by-six-foot banners to be awarded to schools that demonstrated a commitment to the program.

Schools that the library knew were working hard on getting kids signed up were surveyed to determine whether they should be awarded a banner. The school needed to have a minimum enrollment of 250 students and have at least 90 percent of its student population registered for the Power Card. The survey was completed, signed by the school librarian and the principal, and returned to branch staff. There was no "check" on this survey and HPL didn't expect schools to poll students; instead, the library was looking to reward schools that had made a strong effort and achieved results in the Power Card campaign. If a school was not yet at 90 percent, then the survey reminded them, and helped to motivate them to earn their banner. The banner was shown off at area meetings of principals where schools that had achieved 90 percent were mentioned and schools that had not achieved this goal were challenged, not just by the library staff but often by their district supervisor, to get kids signed up for Power Cards.

In most schools, the school librarians were the biggest supporters of the Power Card. Most school librarians saw the Power Card not only as a way to expand their students' access to information, in particular to databases the school could not afford to buy, but also to increase their own visibility in schools. With the strong support of the superintendents and the supervisors of school libraries in every district, school librarians worked long and hard to help get kids registered. Acting on the "challenge" idea, some branch libraries sponsored competitions between schools. For example, the Stanaker Branch Library involved each elementary school in a contest to see who could get the most students registered, with the winning school earning a bright piñata as a prize.

But the real incentive for most school librarians was knowing that, by helping all students in their school to get Power Cards, they were doing the most important job of any school librarian: supporting student achievement. In a message that summarizes many received by HPL staff from school librarians, a librarian from one elementary school wrote:

> I am reporting for Whittier Elementary School. As of November 1998, we have 100% participation in the POWER CARD program. I have just finished collecting the last application—which makes a grand total of 619! Our current enrollment is 596, so our grand total also reflects students who have moved, new students and the children of our staff. Thank you for making this program available to us.—*Jane Robertson, Library Media Specialist, Whittier Elementary*

Although the majority of schools reporting sign-ups of 90 percent or better were elementary schools, several middle schools and one high school (High School for the Performing and Visual Arts) earned a banner. While every branch library served more than one school, the Heights Branch Library was the only one to get every elementary school in its service area a banner. There are many reasons for this, but credit goes primarily to the staff of that branch, in particular children's librarian Mary Wagoner, for networking in the community and motivating school librarians to assist with the Power Card program.

Other school personnel became some of the biggest boosters of the program, thanks in part to active outreach on the part of HPL to make educators aware of the program. Starting with attendance at the HISD Schools of Excellence conference attended by every HISD educator each fall, HPL staff members made numerous presentations about the Power Card. The Power Card was promoted at meetings before HISD's district administrators, various district principals' meetings, reading teacher trainers, the curriculum council, parent educators, and, of course, school library media specialists. Private school librarians, early childhood educators, after-school program providers, and educators from suburban school districts also heard the Power Card message and pledged their support. One outgrowth of the cooperation was the mention of the Power Card in a letter about reading from HISD Superintendent Rod Paige sent to the home of every HISD student in January 1999.

Schools were not the only avenue to reach kids. The library also formed partnerships with a variety of youth and community groups. Such agencies as Girl Scouts, Boy Scouts, Boys and Girls Clubs, Big Brothers and Big Sisters, and the mayor's After School Initiative all helped by distributing applications and/or promoting the Power Card in their publications. In March HPL did a mass mailing to over 350 youth-serving agencies asking them to answer the Power Card Challenge. The mayor's Anti-Gang Task Force supplied the database of agencies to the library. Over 50 percent of the agencies responded by returning the postcard pledging their support and they then received applications to distribute. The library also reached out to the faith community with a mass mailing to church youth groups.

In addition, the library formed important partnerships with other city departments that serve youth. The fire department provided its top personnel, including the fire chief, to be guest readers at special story times. The police department's DARE program handed out applications as part of their presentation at schools. The parks department distributed and collected Power Card applications at its 35 community centers. When a young person registered with the parks department for programs such as youth soccer, the parks included a Power Card application in the registration materials. The park centers would then send the completed applications to the library through the city's interoffice mail. The library would process the applications and mail the cards out within a week. The parks department and city council members host "Fundays in the Park" across the city on spring and summer weekends, and the library set up Power Card sign-up tables at most of these events, as well as a sign-up at the zoo. Another example of interdepartment cooperation is the requirement by the presiding judge of the municipal courts that every youthful offender register for a Power Card before the youth's next scheduled court appearance.

It was the city's health department that provided the library with access to both parents and children, in particular those in underserved neighborhoods. Library staff distributed applications at city health clinics as part of the cooperative Born to Read programs held at those facilities and staff also visited WIC centers. One of the most successful partnerships with the health department occurred as part of the annual immunization drive. As parents stood in long lines at health clinics with their children waiting to get their shots so they could go to school, staff members from the library, with clipboards and applications in hand, were there to make sure that, in addition to having a healthy body, they got a Power Card to build a strong mind. While much of this work was done by key contacts at the branch libraries and health clinics, the health department became the first city department to invite library staff to sign up employees at their center.

The connection between health care providers and the library didn't stop with just the health department. During National Library Week as part of the Power Card Challenge, newborns at local hospitals were presented with Power Card bibs (saying "I'm a Power Baby" in English and Spanish) and a library card application. Focus on younger children was extended with outreach to the local Head Start community. All four Head Start providers were very supportive, allowing for applications to be distributed at centers, and HPL staff were invited to visit centers to do sign-ups during parent nights.

The cultural arts community, in particular the Children's Museum of Houston, also embraced the Power Card Challenge. Through a grant from the Institute of Museums and Libraries, the HPL and the Children's Museum created a Parent Resource Center library at the Children's Museum. The small branch, focusing just on resources for parents and young children, makes Power Card sign-ups at the museum a daily occurrence. In addition, the Children's Museum also sponsored three "Power Card Sundays" where any child with a Power Card received free admission, and those who had not already registered could do so at the library's booth in the museum. The admission was covered by Reliant Energy, who wanted to see organizations like the Children's Museum, which it also supported, support the Power Card. The library also set up booths at the Children's Museum during other events, such as Celebration of the Young Child. The Children's Museum was just one of four museums where the library did registrations during Museum Open House Day. The Museum of Fine Arts utilized a grant to provide free admission to any child with a Power Card on the weekends as part of the program. This "value-added model" from the Museum experience was later utilized in conjunction with a local tourist attraction, the Space Center Houston. Not only did Space Center Houston offer free admission with a Power Card, but it also donated money back to the library. The library also was on hand at Space Center Houston for several days during spring break to sign up visiting parents and their children.

Off-site registration at events turned out to be one of the most successful strategies for achieving the Power Card goals. Recognizing that "kids will be kids" and that many applications never made it home, the library made a new commitment to outreach, with well over 500 outreach events taking place during the first year of the program. The most successful events were the large citywide festivals. Sign-ups at the Power of Houston, the Houston Rodeo and Livestock Show, the Children's Festival, and the International Festival during the first year of the program netted over 1,000 completed applications. In the fall of 1988 the library set up booths as part of a local grocery store chain (Fiesta) literacy program, then returned to Fiesta stores in the spring in partnership with ServeHouston, the local AmeriCorps agency that provided volunteers to help with registration. A similar program in the fall of 1989 with Kroger stores was not as successful, in part because unlike Fiesta, whose stores primarily served city residents, Kroger was located further out in suburban communities. The "push" to parents and children in the suburbs was more difficult, so the library developed a "script" for those doing outreach. The script highlighted the databases that could be accessed for free to complete homework via the library's Web page; it also emphasized the attraction of visiting the Central Library's children's department during trips downtown to visit museums or to attend baseball games at the new downtown stadium.

The library did off-site registration at educational conferences, community meetings, political functions, neighborhood festivals, Little League sign-up, career days, job fairs, town hall meetings, home schooling conferences, adult education graduation ceremonies, malls, department stores, movie theaters, and health fairs. The library was on hand for such special events as the mayor's

Youth Celebration, the city employee health fairs, and numerous community celebrations, like National Night Out. Some events required staff from just one branch, while others became regional activities. For big events, staff was recruited from throughout the whole system. These big events provided staff from across the system and at many different levels with an opportunity to work together on a project to meet the goals of the library. While there were many success stories from outreach, there were also plenty of disappointments as expected crowds did not show up and/or the community partner did not follow through on pledges to promote and support the program. Over the course of the Power Card Challenge, library staff learned which types of events provided the best use of resources and how best to staff and run a booth. Staff got very experienced at putting together an outreach box containing applications, library maps, bookmarks, pencils, library cards, and a wide variety of literature about programs and services.

For example, early on staff realized that people need a reason, especially at a large festival, to stop by the library booth. Soon the Power Card Wheel was born. Constructed to be first used during National Library Week in 1999, this large wheel contained different colors and numbers. People came up, gave the wheel a spin, and then had chances to answer questions and win incentives. The wheel was used not only at outreach events, but also within the library. Because of its size, it was not easily moved, so one of the region work teams developed a small version which would fit in someone's car. The library also developed a cardboard "stand-up" of Mayor Brown holding up a library card with one hand and extending his other hand. This was rolled out at a sign-up at the office of Reliant Energy where anyone signing up for a card had the chance to have his or her picture taken with "the mayor." It was also used, along with bright banners, to attract attention. Eventually the library used gift money to purchase a large Power Card tent, which could be used at outdoor events to keep staff and library card applicants out of the elements while they completed the registration process.

The off-site registration was a low-tech affair, not only because the library lacked a sufficient number of laptops on which to load registration software, but also mostly because the business at these outreach events was fast and furious. Often over 100 people would visit a booth staffed by one or two people during an hour. Rather than adding the database record at the sign-up table, a more efficient procedure was adopted. Once an application was completed, the customer was handed a new library card along with a brochure (available in both English and Spanish) explaining the loan policies, fines, and so on. On the application, the staff person wrote the bar code number of the issued card but the applicant was told not to use the card for three to five days. At the end of the outreach session, the completed applications were returned to a circulation desk to be processed. After the card number and relevant information were entered into the database, kids were ready to start powering up their cards and checking out materials.

HOW IS THE LIBRARY PROMOTING THE POWER CARD?

At these outreach events, a large number of parents and kids said, "Oh, the Power Card, I've heard about that!" To promote the Power Card, the library's public information officer Sheryl Berger developed a far-reaching media strategy to ensure that every Houstonian heard about the Power Card. The first important media event was a kickoff press conference held in late July. The press conference included remarks by Mayor Brown, Library Director Gubbin, as well as representatives from Reliant Energy and HISD. The press conference was also heavy on youth involvement. Not only was the press conference "stage" area covered with kids wearing orange Power Card T-shirts, but one of the young customers in attendance, a high school student, made remarks urging other youth to get their Power Cards.

The press conference was covered by most Houston TV stations, including a long piece on one of the Spanish-language stations. The conference also led to a large article in the city's only daily newspaper, the *Houston Chronicle,* followed by a strong editorial in the Sunday paper urging parents to get their kids Power Cards. While Houston only has one major daily newspaper, the metro area is home to lots of small suburban newspapers as well as those serving ethnic markets. The library was able to place stories about the Power Card in many of these papers on a regular basis. In addition, the library placed press releases about the Power Card in school newsletters, community newsletters, PTA newsletters, neighborhood association newsletters, and employee newsletters. Some school newspapers even ran stories about the Power Card program.

The press conference was taped for the municipal channel and was run repeatedly over the next few months. Invited to the press conference were community partners, representatives for other school districts, and other potential Power Card supporters. Not only did those covering the press conference receive a press kit packed with information about the library and the Power Card Challenge, but the press also received photos a few weeks later of the activities as well as more information. Throughout the course of the program, media would receive updates on the status of the program. In addition, the Power Card was highlighted not just on the municipal channel, but also on HISD's educational station which ran a long story on the Power Card press conference.

Watching all this coverage from the wings were lots and lots of library staff members. Memos and e-mail messages had been sent, and meetings had been held about the Power Card, but for most staff, especially those at the Central Library, this was their first exposure to how huge a campaign was in the works. For some staff, the press conference was a turning point: this wasn't just "another program" that would be announced and then forgotten (as often happens in all library systems), but something that was real and would have impact. Once again, while the primary aim of a Power Card event was to get the word out to the public, the secondary function of motivating staff was just as important.

In addition to speeches at the press conference by the mayor and others, a highlight of the press conference was the unveiling of two large billboards—one in English, one in Spanish—showing the Power Card. Over 200 of these billboards, which were donated by Eller Media, were placed in strategic locations around the city, and each branch library received one to display. Another key feature of the press conference was the performance of the High Impact Squad, a group of performers who dress up in "super hero" costumes and perform death-defying basketball dunks. The Library hired the High Impact Squad in 2001, the final year of the program, through a grant from the Carnegie Foundation, to perform at schools and other functions to promote the Power Card message. Video of the High Impact Squad performing and of a group of young people decked out in orange T-shirts and showing off their new Power Cards became the central images for a public service announcement (PSA) produced by Warner Cable. The mayor also participated in shooting a PSA which was aired more than 200 times on Warner Cable.

The media strategy also included library staff taking the Power Card message to the airwaves. Staff were interviewed on local TV and radio stations, including several interviews with the Spanish-language media. Media partnerships were key, as radio and TV stations donated airtime to run the PSAs. One television station (Channel 13) helped fund Power Card book jackets as part of its Kids First campaign, while the local Fox and UPN affiliates moved from being Power Card sponsors to becoming sponsors of the library's summer reading programs. Public radio and television were huge supporters of the Power Card and often did stories about the library. The library was even invited one evening to answer phones for the PBS station. Viewers tuned in and saw an ocean of orange shirts and heard interviews with library staff, including Library Director Gubbin, about the Power Card.

Commercial partners also helped promote the Power Card. For example, McDonald's in the Houston area joined with the library to produce special tray mats promoting the Power Card. Reliant Energy followed up its initial mailing with a later one, this one promoting the partnership with the Children's Museum of Houston. Cynthia Cooper, star of the WNBA Houston Comets, helped promote the Power Card through her Roopster Roux literacy program. The library began receiving calls from other groups wanting to get involved: the Power Card—because of the mayor's support, the involvement of Reliant, and the success of the "hype" surrounding it—was seen as a winner.

Some of the more successful outreach events, such as visits to school on the night of open houses sponsored by the parent-teacher associations, were held in conjunction with commercial partners. At these events, library staff not only had a chance to register students and parents for cards, but also to tell parents about all the resources now available to their children with a Power Card. Many outreach opportunities emerged because of networking and leveraging prior relationships. For example, the Houston Astros had long supported HPL's summer reading program with free tickets as incentives, but they extended that partnership by inviting the library to participate in a special "fan fest" at Enron Field. Similarly, the library was well networked with local educational organizations and used those connections to set up registration booths. In the fall and spring, the library had a booth at the Houston Area Educators of Young Children's conferences. These events did not directly yield a large number of youth registrations, but all those in attendance were adults involved in the education of young children in the community. At the outreach session, the library provided these educators with stacks of applications, contacts to arrange library visits, and other information about services the library could offer them. While the purpose of most outreach was sign-up, it served a secondary purpose: to show the community that the library is actively involved in supporting the education of children. From visits to schools to booths at community events, the Houston area learned a great deal about the library and the Power Card when they saw staff in those bright orange shirts.

The visual aspect of the Power Card—with its bright colors— was an important part of the promotion strategy. Photos from the press conference were quickly transformed into a series of promotional products, including a Power Point presentation, display boards for use at outreach, and the Power Card Web page. The Power Card Web page (*www.hpl.lib.tx.us/powercard*) was a focal point in promoting the Power Card, not only to the community at large, but also to library staff. The page was updated with the latest information about the program, but more importantly updated with photos from Power Card events. The library purchased disposable cameras for each branch to use to document their activities. The Power Card Web page was loaded with pictures of kids holding up their Power Cards, of staff out in the community, and of staff rallying around the "Power Tower." The Power Tower documented sign-ups as the "critter" moved up a stack of books each month. The Power Tower, located in the lobby of the Central Library, provided a striking visual image letting the public "see" how the library was doing in reaching the mayor's goal. Just as striking was the larger Power Card logo painted during the final year of the program on each of the library's delivery vans, which were, on occasion, used in community parades. Although the project to get the vans painted was coordinated by the Power Card project manager, Gail Hicks, the idea, like so many other good ones, came from a staff member working a circulation desk.

Another part of the promotion for the Power Card was to increase the quantity and the quality of programming as a way to motivate children and their parents to visit the library. Under the direction of the manager of programs, Janine Golden, the library started new celebrations, such as programming for Teen Read Week, Read Across America Day, Kids Online Week, and Cinco de Mayo celebrations, as well as expanding programs during National Children's Book Week, National Library Week, and during the summer reading program. During the first year of the Power Card, beginning in December and lasting through May, there was a Power Card program at each branch library. At the Central Library and several branches, the program took the form of an open house. At several branches, these open houses became huge community celebrations, complete with food, entertainment, games, and book sales, as well as library card sign-ups. The purpose of all the Power Card programs was to increase awareness of the library in the community, to partner with community groups to produce a program, and finally to celebrate the Power Card.

While these programs did divert some staff energy and resources toward an in-library program rather than toward outreach, the goal was for each branch to have its own "kickoff" like the one held at the HPL central library.

A second press conference, combined with a donor recognition breakfast, was held in August 2000 to kick off the second year of the Power Card campaign. Mayor Brown again spoke, as did other community representatives, about the success of the first year and the goals for the second year of the program. But more important, the Central Library lobby was bedecked with streamers in the Power Card colors and with plenty of orange balloons. Unveiled at the donor breakfast were large banners listing the names of the corporations, schools, agencies, and city departments that contributed to the success of the campaign. These donors were again honored in slick library annual reports, produced with the assistance of Reliant Energy, which were distributed in the community. Reliant Energy also paid for the production of the "Popcorn Piece," a slick poster-sized report which went to all sponsors and staff. Attached to the report was a bag of microwave popcorn, another small reward to celebrate the end of the second year of the program.

The Power Card Challenge program officially ended on August 28, 2001, with a press conference held by Mayor Brown and Library Director Gubbin outlining the successes of the previous three years.

The Power Card branding—the logo, the typeface, and especially the bright orange color—served as excellent tools for creating a wide range of products and incentives. The incentives, such as a Power Card basket stuffed with goodies raffled off each month in branches in the Collier region, were used in the libraries to increase circulation. During the final year of the program, at the recommendations of the newly formed Power Card work teams, the library dedicated resources to incentives to give to patrons. In many cases, these incentives were given away at outreach visits in the community to children and adults who signed up for cards. Power Card cups, pencils, stickers, and tattoos were produced as incentives. With the support of the Friends of the Library, the library also purchased incentives for staff, such as caps, lanyards, and lapel pins. In addition, each regional work team received funding from the Friends of the Library to purchase their own incentives for staff and customers. Customers could also get into the act; for example, in the third year of the Power Card program, the library offered for sale bright orange Power Card T-shirts and watches. Power Card watches and T-shirts were also used as incentives in the library's summer reading program.

HOW DID THE LIBRARY STAFF ANSWER THE POWER CARD CHALLENGE?

The enthusiasm of the Power Card program was contagious. Once a month, library staff was asked to don orange T-shirts for Power Card dress-up days. Early in the program, various Central Library departments posed decked out in their shirts for group photos. A staff photo contest was held for pictures of staff wearing their Power Card T-shirts in a wide variety of places: from one librarian showing off her shirt while on a visit to Mexico, to another one wearing it on stage when playing with her rock band. Although taken after the contest, one of the most striking of all staff photos is that of Coulette and Joan, two of the library's juvenile services librarians, posing with their shirts on the Great Wall of China. Staff wore the shirts in the library, at outreach sessions, and *any* place they would attract attention. With the bright orange color, the shirts always attracted attention.

In February 2001 the orange shirts were "retired" and replaced with a brand new "mellow yellow" staff shirt bearing the Power Card logo on the front and Reliant Energy's logo on the sleeve. Several of the region work teams also produced their own shirts, such as the "High Voltage Squad" of the Collier region's blue-and-yellow shirts, or the purple shirts from the Scenic Woods region. On dress-up days, however, some staff members do not wear orange T-shirts; they wear the white or gray Power Card polo shirts. These staff are members of the library's "Polo Club" which recognizes outstanding individual achievements and creative ideas to support the program.

One of the first members of the Polo Club was Lena, who worked in the Central Library's business, science, and technology department. Lena asked if she could do a sign-up at her daughter's school in the Klein School District. She so enjoyed the positive feedback she received from the community that she volunteered to take the Power Card to other Klein schools. Lena soon became one of the most active members of the entire staff, always thinking of new ways and new places to promote the Power Card. Janet in the facilities department handed out Power Card applications to children in her church and asked children who came to her house to sell candy if they had Power Cards. Al in the Houston Area Library System office and other members of his department walked their neighborhoods handing out applications. The Polo Club served as just one method by which the library sought to recognize its "power staff." Reliant Energy conveyed its thanks to the staff by purchasing pizza for every branch and department during the summer of 1999 to celebrate the first year of the program.

The second year brought about the "Blue Crew," when the Friends of the Library purchased denim shirts with the Power Card logo. The second year of the campaign also brought about a major shift in the structure of the campaign, with each region as well as the Central Library developing work teams. These work teams became, within their regions, the cheerleaders for the program. The teams coordinated staffing large outreach events, organized parties and other staff functions, helped share resources and ideas, and, each month, nominated one person from their work area to be named to the "Blue Crew." The library maintained a "Blue Crew" Web page linked from the Power Card page, so that staff could see their names and good deeds on the Web, and the rest of the staff could learn who was being honored and why.

During the third year of the program, rather than rewarding individuals, the focus was on groups, departments, or work teams. Once a month, the Power Card steering committee would select a team to pose for a picture in front of the Power Tower along with Library Director Barbara Gubbin. A real effort was employed to reward the staff members working behind the scenes to make the Power Card happen. For example, one of the first photos taken was of Gubbin with the drivers of the vans that carried books between branches. Because of the Power Card, this group's workload had increased tremendously—they moved the onslaught of Power Card applications and other documents around the system, the increase in circulation led to more books moving from branch to branch, and increased book budgets led to more new books being transported to the branch libraries. The picture was another small but significant way of recognizing their achievement.

Just as the Power Card program has provided the library with a focus for its promotion, programming, and outreach, it has served as a jumping-off point for staff to "show their stuff." All staff, not just those in children's libraries, are contributing ideas, energy, and enthusiasm. Leila at the Robinson-Westchase Branch Library dressed up the stuffed animals in her children's area with Power Card T-shirts, while staff from across the system have created and decorated themselves with Power Card earrings, bracelets, buttons, ribbons, and hats with the Power Card logo. Nora from the Pleasantville Branch Library turned her creative energy to music and developed a Power Card rap which she used at schools to promote the program. This led the library to hold a

Power Card rap contest from its Power Card Web page and Nora won the library's branch-employee-of-the-year award. Staff at the Moody Branch Library decorated a car with Power Card colors for use in a community National Night Out parade. Children's librarians John and Sandy coordinated a project to order Power Card watches for staff, while Janie from the Jungman Branch Library provided "powerful" ribbons for staff doing outreach. Betty at the Smith Branch Library became known as the Power Card queen for her inventive ways of promoting the program.

During the first two years of the program, information about the Power Card was provided to staff through a variety of methods. Time at branch staff meetings was dedicated to reviewing Power Card activities, while all managers' meetings featured a Power Card update. Lots of information was sent out via e-mail, often referring staff to the Power Card Web page for more information. Communication became more formalized during the second and third years of the program, with a printed Power Card report sent monthly to each unit. The report promoted all of the month's outreach events and branch programs, listed the next dress-up day, and reported on the progress toward the Power Card goals. A Power Card listserv was organized to send information about the program, as well as report successes and request volunteers for outreach events.

The Power Card Challenge began as a very top-down project, with the Power Card steering committee (made up of the library's assistant director, the chief of technical services, the programming manager, the public information officer, the marketing director, and the manager of youth programs) setting the agenda for all staff. A few months after the program began, a project manager, Fred Schumacher, was hired to oversee the day-to-day operations of the program, develop new programs and partnerships, and carry out projects determined by the steering committee. After a retreat in the spring of 1999 (attended by the steering committee and a cross-section of staff members representing branches, Central Library departments, and support departments), however, the work team concept was born and staff began to take more ownership of the program. The work teams would consisted of all types of staff, from branch managers to desk clerks. The work teams provided staff with an opportunity to set the agenda, share information, and reward accomplishment. Each branch and every Central Library department was asked to produce a work plan on projects they would undertake to meet the Power Card goals. Those work plans were then coordinated by the work teams for each region to share resources.

To prepare for the final year of the Power Card, another retreat was held in May 2000, inviting the leaders of all the work teams as well as other staff from across the system to plan for the final year. In addition, a staff survey was conducted to determine what staff felt was and was not working in meeting the goals. The final year of the program had no work plans, but rather a best practices document. The best practices demonstrated that the library was becoming a "learning organization" in that staff members were able to identify the most effective and efficient ways of doing the Power Card program and also correct mistakes and missteps. Those best practices were divided into the major areas of concern, and then "assigned" to a certain level of responsibility, ranging from best practices to be utilized by the members of the steering committee to those to be practiced by all staff. The retreat ended with each person in attendance signing the Power Card banner and pledging his or her support for the final year of the Power Card. The signed banner was then brought to meetings of managers, youth librarians, and others to sign and commit to supporting the program.

WHAT ARE THE OUTCOMES OF THE POWER CARD CHALLENGE?

The most tangible outcomes of the Power Card program are the achievement of the library's goals for the first year of the Power Card—having 200,000 active juvenile library cardholders and increasing juvenile circulation by 20 percent. The library ended its fiscal year on June 30, 1999, with 204,183 kids with cards. There was a huge jump in registrations in the fall from the initial "buzz" about the program, and then another jump in the spring when outreach hit full stride. The second goal was also met with a juvenile circulation increase of 21 percent. Progress toward the circulation goal started slowly, but, with the addition of videos at each branch library, an influx of juvenile paperbacks, as well as a new emphasis on merchandising collections, circulation exploded in the spring.

The following year, the library smashed its registration goal by more than 15 percent, ending the year with 277,807 holders of a Power Card. Although the circulation goal fell short, the library did increase its overall juvenile circulation to over three million items during the second full year of the Power Card. In the third year, a variety of circumstances, including critical staffing shortages, branch closings for renovation, and a major natural disaster striking the city in the final month of the campaign, led the library to fall just short of both its circulation and registration goals. The registration goal of 303,000 active youth library cardholders was short by just 95 new youth library cardholders.

For the purposes of the Power Card campaign, the registration goal was always just youth registration, although adult registration also increased dramatically. One major element affecting the registration goal was that the number represented active borrowers. Thus, even as new library cardholders were being signed up each month, others who had not used their cards in three years were falling off. The library did not offer to waive past fines (as some libraries do during card campaigns), so perhaps many young people who might have wanted a new Power Card were unable to obtain one due to past fines that they could not afford to pay. An effort to send postcards to customers whose cards were about to expire to motivate them to reregister did not achieve a great deal of success. This happened, in part, because Houston is a very mobile city and cardholders were no longer at the same address. Even though the final goals of the program were not met, the Power Card Challenge exceeded the expectations of almost everyone associated with it in many other ways.

Houston Public Library was honored when the Texas Library Association named the Power Card Challenge the 1998 "Program of the Year" for demonstrating excellence in school cooperation, community outreach, media support, government backing, and staff involvement. As the award was announced, the library staff in attendance leapt to their feet, each of them wearing a Power Card T-shirt. The Power Card Challenge also won the 2000 John Cotton Dana Award from the American Library Association. Reliant Energy was named the "Library Philanthropist of the Year" by the Texas Library Association in 2000 for that corporation's dedication to the Power Card; Reliant also received an award for the design of the Power Card from a graphic design association.

The support of Mayor Brown, his administration, and the Houston City Council has been crucial to the success of the program. For his support, Mayor Brown was named in the September 1998 issue of *Library Journal* as one of "Six Politicians Who Made a Difference" and he was named *Library Journal*'s "Politician of the Year" in September 1999. The mayor consistently mentions the Power Card in his speeches, both in the city and at national conferences. The Power Card became a centerpiece of his administration which focuses on neighborhoods and youth. A picture of the mayor holding the Power Card was featured on the cover of a directory of all youth programs offered by the city and a commercial featuring the Power Card was used in his successful reelection campaign in 1999. The mayor's youth council also signed on to promote the Power Card and helped coordinate sign-ups in their schools. City council members as well helped promote the Power Card in their districts.

The Power Card's positive outcomes for the library are numerous. Not only has the program earned it recognition, but the program also became a foundation on which to build. While the library had for years been moving toward more community involvement and partnerships, the Power Card fast-tracked that strategy. From the relationship with Reliant Energy which committed to support the program for three years, to the media partnerships, to the partnerships created at the local branch level, the Power Card has been a powerful tool of cooperation, communication, and consistent improvement in the quality and quantity of library services offered to the residents of Houston. In the midst of the success of the Power Card, the library next launched into a strategic planning process focusing on the need to renovate buildings and create a new central library. While such planning was inevitable, the Power Card gave the library administration confidence that it had support in the community. The Power Card showed the community what the library could do and what it could be. The *Houston Press*, an alternative weekly paper, went so far as to call the Power Card "the best thing any government agency has done for anybody in a long time."

CONCLUSION

Because of the Power Card Challenge, not only do more kids have cards, but also those kids have more programs, they have more materials, and they are the primary focus of HPL's attention. Parents, teachers, and caregivers are impacted as kids gain more access to information. The Houston community benefits because "kids who read succeed" and the project is creating more library users and readers. The increased visibility in the community and the support of city government positively impact the library as an institution. The library benefits as more staff is added, more materials and equipment are purchased, and more cooperation occurs. Schools, community organizations, and businesses are impacted as partnerships are formed with HPL. The impact is citywide, yet it also comes down to the individual child who, as Mayor Brown promised, is empowered by getting, then using, a Power Card. Or as one young person wrote in a Power Card rap:

It's the P-O-W-E-R-C-A-R-D
PowerPacked with a capital P
It's the key to many places held by me
So when I want to check out a book rain or shine
I'll use the Power Card and it'll be just fine
I'll just open up a book and use my imagination
And I can travel to any place all across the nation
It's the coolest thing and the new sensation

See the "Gallery of Successful Library Card Campaign Programs" for these documents from the Houston Public Library:

√ Power Card Application (English)
√ Power Card Application (Spanish)
√ Power Card Report
√ Power Card Express
√ Pack the Power Brochure
√ Power Card Postcard

4 PHILADELPHIA FREEDOM: THE LIBRARY CARD CAMPAIGN OF THE PHILADELPHIA FREE LIBRARY

One of the pictures featured in *American Libraries* to mark the first national library card sign-up shows Philadelphia Mayor W. Wilson Goode and the Free Library of Philadelphia (FLP) Director Elliott Shelkrot holding up the "The Best Gift You'll Ever Give Your Child" poster. The photo came from a session at city hall where Mayor Goode proclaimed October 9, 1987, to be "Library Card Sign-Up Day" in Philadelphia and urged all parents to "help their children acquire library cards." What began in 1987 as a one-day affair emerged a dozen years later as a three-phase, year-long campaign involving the Free Library of Philadelphia system's 50 branches, 3 regional libraries, and the Central Library, all of which provide library service to the citizens of the city. Philadelphia is a city of approximately 1.5 million, with a good portion of that population being children and teens. According to census figures, the population includes 118,764 teens (12 to 17 years), 126,294 school-age children (6 to 11 years), and 117,199 preschoolers (birth to 5 years). The teens and school-age children attend 438 public, charter, parochial, and private schools. The schools know the library well, as it is the responsibility of the adult/teen and children's librarians of FLP to visit each school assigned to their agency twice a year to promote library services.

There were three separate phases of the Free Library of Philadelphia registration drive. In August 1999 there were 455,159 borrowers. Before beginning the fall 1999 campaign the Free Library set a goal of "500,000 in 2000"— 500,000 borrowers in force by the end of the century. On December 31, at the end of the fall 2000 drive, the Free Library had 506,890 cards in the hands of library users. The success of the three initiatives (described below) is, according to the library administration, almost entirely due to the human factor. From the wide representation on the crossdivisional task force (which helped create active support from library departments not directly involved in public service work), to the day-in, day-out hard work of all staff to motivate kids to get cards, through the actual processing of the cards, it was a "high-touch" campaign. The crusading of one School District of Philadelphia administrator to register all kindergartners caught the attention of others who didn't want their students to miss the opportunity to obtain a library, or lose out on the chance to win a computer. However, above all, the administration of the library directly attributes the success of the initiatives to the enthusiasm and commitment of FLP public service staff on all levels who developed creative ways to approach schools, organizations, businesses, and other interesting venues to promote library services and register individuals. While the materials attracted attention and the computers and other giveaways offered incentives, the library staff "sold" the campaign.

A task force that met on a regular basis managed all three phases of the campaign. The campaign was conducted under the direction of Associate Director Kathy Gosliner. The task force included representatives from communication and development, extensions, the central public services division, information technology, the volunteer office, the Friends of the Free Library, and the office of public service support (TOPSS) units of the library. All of these units were involved in one or more aspects of the campaign. During the first year, a smaller team met weekly as well. A review of recent statistics—systemwide and branch-by-branch—was part of almost all meetings. Mary Flournoy, young adult specialist in the office of public service support, and Linda Fein, an area administrator in the extension division, served as cochairs of the task force. The library card campaign involved almost every agency and unit of FLP. During Phase One (students in K–12), several staff meetings were held to communicate about the library card campaign and the other changes involving registration procedures. They included a meeting for representatives of all branches and departments as well as follow-up area meetings for branch heads. Staff focus groups were held to plan for Phase Two (adults) and Phase Three (specific grades). After each task force meeting, updates on the campaign were distributed to staff via e-mail.

PHASE 1—FALL 1999

The first phase of the library card campaign focused on school children (K–12) in all schools: public, private, parochial, and charter. Because a lot of systemwide initiatives were happening at the same time (including a new institutional logo, designed by an outside firm, which created a need for a new library card design and finding a new vendor for the cards), there was very little time to do long-range planning or get input from frontline staff. At the same time, the children's and adult/young adult application was merged into one and the age for young adult was lowered from 14 to 12. In addition, the library had recently obtained access to (and approval to use) the School District of Philadelphia's database of student names and home addresses. Because these initiatives had to be in place before the registration drive could begin, many decisions had to be made in a short amount of time.

At the request of Stephanie Childs, the head of the Office of Kindergarten Support of the School District of Philadelphia (SDP), the library quickly prepared special applications/letters to kindergarten parents to be sent to each school. The letters were packed by library volunteers in large envelopes for each school, with return envelopes labeled for the Office of Kindergarten Support. They were to be given to the parents when they came for a mandatory meeting with the teacher before kindergarten started. Parents were asked to return the applications to the teacher who would send completed applications to the kindergarten office where a Free Library staff member picked them up. The library also modified the design of a library coloring book to include a special welcome and a list of all the branches on the back, and used the bear from the coloring book in a special library card holder and envelope. The coloring book was given to the kindergarten children when they came into the branch to use their new cards for the first time. Libraries also requested these materials in quantities to use for drives at private and parochial kindergartens.

A designer was hired to produce brochures targeted to grades 1–6 and grades 7–12. One was mailed directly to the homes of students in Philadelphia public and charter schools. Since the library already had the database of names and addresses for these students, these brochures did not include an application form. The grade 1–6 brochure included spaces for a parent/guardian to give permission for his or her child to have a card and to indicate whether the parent/guardian authorized open access to the entire collection. Students were invited to come in to their local library to "activate" or "upgrade" their cards and to be automatically entered into a contest to win a computer. Two similar brochures were designed with an application for a Free Library card; these brochures were to be taken by FLP librarians to the private and parochial schools in the city.

Alternative Work Environments (AWE), the library's technology vendor, graciously donated three computers for this campaign—one for a "winner" from grades 1–6; one for a "winner" from grades 7–12; and a laptop for the Teen Leadership Assistant (a high school aide in the library's after-school program) who signed up the most people for a library card. McDonald's donated coupons for ice cream cones for the elementary students who came in to get a new card and the Philadelphia Coca-Cola Bottling Co. donated coupons for Dasani bottled water for the teens. These coupons were obtained through the efforts of staff in the FLP development office. This office also began contacting corporate funders and board members, offering to set up library card drives at their offices.

The kickoff was held in October 1999, during Teen Read Week, with a parade of 100 teens. The SDP superintendent was one of the speakers. As a high school band played, a big banner was unfurled from the balcony of the Central Library announcing the campaign. The campaign was featured on a morning TV news show, since the host of the show also spoke at the kickoff. The kickoff was featured on many radio stations during the fall. Radio stations that have teen audiences ran public service announcements (PSAs) that featured teens talking about the Free Library. In November a special Children's Book Week activity was polling children at four libraries about their favorite book. A costumed character, Franklin the Turtle, was a featured guest at an event announcing the favorite books, while a Pokemon costumed character was a special guest at a Philadelphia READS event for 50 elementary principals/administrators. All 50 had their picture taken with the Pokemon character and a big library card. One of the principals took a pad of applications back to his school for his faculty members. A special application form was given to that school later for use in a parent's newsletter.

The winners of the two donated computers were chosen at random by computer. Both the first-grade girl and the seventh-grade boy (a recent Haitian immigrant and first-time cardholder) were thrilled. The winning Teen Library Assistant earned a computer by signing up 228 people for library cards. In October 1999, the *Philadelphia Daily News* printed a supplement on the Free Library, including a library card application which could be taken to an agency, mailed, or faxed.

In addition to the direct-mail effort, the library staff ventured out to all sorts of community events (such as children's theater productions) for library card registrations. A new venue for library card registrations was city council hearings at City Hall; staff members from Central Library departments staffed the tables. In addition to getting new registrations, an effort was made to get everyone reapplied for a card. Since the FLP card expires after three years, each month there are patrons whose cards expire. A special effort was made to bring those with expired cards back into the fold. The library's information technology (IT) department designed a form letter for patrons in good standing whose cards had expired in the last year. The letter informed them that their cards would be automatically renewed. Since the envelopes had "return service requested," IT received corrected addresses for those who had moved. The application was also put on the FLP Web site for people to print out and then fax or mail in.

From October 15, 1999, through April 1, 2000, over 30,000 young people registered for library cards or had their cards "upgraded." A breakdown of those registrants by age level is shown in the following table:

Grade Level	# of Registrants
Kindergarten	3,712
Grades 1–6	13,917
Grades 7–12	12,698
Total	30,327

Only one branch did not have an increase in the number of borrowers; all but 3 branches (out of 50) had an increase of at least 3 percent. One branch reported an increase of 75 percent in registrations. Not only had the branch recently been renovated, but also it was in a brand-new community center building. Furthermore, it also featured a complete collection of materials for adults and young adults, as previously it had been a children's branch.

The campaign provided the library with the opportunity to overcome many challenges and obstacles in terms of materials, communication to both staff and public, and procedures. The campaign resulted in the lowering of the age level for teens (from 14 to 12) and the development of a new general library card application (one long form as opposed to a green form for children and a short, white form for adults). One of the largest obstacles, however, could not have been avoided: a hurricane, which postponed the meeting/rally to introduce the campaign to staff.

PHASE 2—WINTER/SPRING 2000

The second phase focused on adults and began with a focus group of adult librarians from branches, regional libraries, and Central Library departments in December 1999. Topics discussed included:

- Which special groups or constituencies would each branch or department choose to target for an adult registration campaign?
- What materials would each branch and department need or want from the library system?
- What theme(s) should be used to target adults?
- What publicity materials should the library produce for the campaign?
- What methods could be best utilized to communicate with staff?
- What are the best times and locations to engage in the outreach?

The focus group suggested that the message for the adult campaign stress the fact that the library is a real bargain and has a variety of services to offer people. A librarian from the South Philadelphia Branch Library mentioned that he had developed a very simple flyer to promote all the special materials available at his branch—for *free*! Other good ideas suggested by the group included buttons for the staff to wear, posters to post at a registration site to advertise an upcoming registration drive, a coupon for Friends of the Free Library book sales, press coverage involving the mayor, and a promotional banner for each library to use at outreach events.

Because each branch and department is unique and serves different constituencies, the library administration thought it was important to allow each unit to develop an outreach work plan that was targeted to its unique communities or service areas. The key groups identified by branches were houses of worship, seniors, businesses, and people who work in the community. Central Library departments targeted college students and faculty, local corporations, seniors, and people coming to the library for other reasons, such as attending programs or obtaining tax forms.

A recently retired librarian was hired to be the part-time coordinator of the adult campaign. Her duties included working with the registration drive task force and one of the library's graphic designers to develop the text and design for the campaign materials. She also contacted a number of companies, businesses, and institutions to set up on-site library card registrations or to get materials to them for distribution with employee paychecks. Some college students were hired as outreach assistants and they helped staff with the registrations as well as sending materials to the branches.

Based on the advice of the focus group and the South Philadelphia Branch librarian's flyer advertising the branch, three brochures were developed with the theme "How much would you pay for . . . computers, Internet access, bestsellers, children's books, videos, CD's." The brochures were targeted to the key groups identified by branch staff. One brochure was sized to fit into a mailing envelope; one was sized to fit into bulletins given out at houses of worship (the "house of worship" brochure); another was targeted to seniors, with an application in large print. All were printed with a return address so they could be mailed back to the library. Two bookmarks were prepared: one listing general resources (including parenting information) and one listing resources for seniors (special services for seniors and books for grandchildren). At the time, the library had no formal printed library card materials in Spanish, yet Philadelphia has a large Spanish population. With the help of a library school student from the University of Pittsburgh and several staff members, a Spanish bookmark, application, and disk with a press release in Spanish highlighting our services to the city's Latino community were prepared. Thus, the library card campaign not only motivated citizens to take action by getting a card, it also provided the push for the library to do something: create more materials in Spanish. Other materials included posters alerting people to an on-site library card registration and banners with the new library logo for all branches to use at outreach events. Badges with the slogan "Carry the Card!" were designed for staff and volunteers working at outreach events. Coupons offering 10 percent discount in the Friends of the Free Library Used Book Store were printed and given out at registration drives or mailed with the cards. Library card holders and envelopes with the "Carry the Card!" slogan were also developed.

PECO Energy donated the printing of the general adult and senior bookmarks. A solicitation drive to area companies conducted by FLP's development office resulted in $13,500 from the Center for Applied Research, FMC Corporation, Philadelphia Federal Credit Union, and Sunoco. PECO, SmithKline Beecham (now GlaxoSmithKline), and other corporate donors to the library held library card registrations at their sites. Also, the development office offered a registration drive to the companies of all new members of the library's board of directors. PGW (Philadelphia Gas Works) agreed to put a small, colorful insert into bills. People filled out the insert, sent it to the library, and a prestamped application brochure was sent to them. This idea came from the West Philadelphia regional librarian, who hosted a breakfast for area businesses. As a result of the PGW inserts, 450 applications were requested.

Philadelphia's new mayor, John Street, held a series of town meetings in various areas of the city in November and December 1999. Library staff were there to register people; 78 people signed up at one town meeting alone. At other town meetings, most people already had cards, but they stopped by the registration table to tell library staff what a great service the library provides. The FLP volunteer office had several enthusiastic volunteers who staffed registration tables at the library's "Rebuilding the Future" author lecture series. Some volunteers even approached people who were waiting for the author to sign books to remind them that, even though they lived outside the city, they were eligible for Free Library cards if they worked in the city. Many companies agreed to hold on-site library card drives, and some posted articles in staff newsletters or via e-mail. More than 350 people attending the annual job fair at the Central Library signed up for cards.

All FLP branches and departments were involved in outreach events—at civic associations, hospitals, transit stations, U.S. Airways headquarters at the airport, senior centers, and businesses. Many Central Library departments became more involved in outreach activities as a result of the campaign. For example, the art department staff registered people at special events held at local galleries. The department head suggested a bookmark listing the services of the art department. She also borrowed a five-foot tall enlargement of a woodcut of Van Dyck from the print and picture department on which she pasted a large library card. Van Dyck escorted her on all of her outreach efforts in the city.

April was designated Free Library Card Registration Month. There was a city council proclamation, and the official kickoff occurred on April 1 at the reopening of the Whitman Branch Library. Throughout the month, there were special drives with celebrity guests—at the fire department with the fire commissioner and at the district attorney's office with the DA. All the celebrities posed for a picture with a huge library card. Other drives were held during National Library Week. People signed up for library cards at a supermarket singles' night and at the big weekend book sale sponsored by the Friends of the Free Library. The library paid for advertising on seven radio stations during the week and requested the stations to play them as PSAs afterward.

The local ABC affiliate volunteered to prepare a PSA featuring Mayor Street saying "I Carry the Card. Do you?" and then sent tapes to *all* the other television stations. The library's communications department sent basic information on the campaign to the four library area coordinators on a disk, so that they could add information on their area's local activities for the month and send the information to local papers in their area of the city.

By the end of June 2000, the Free Library had 490,366 registrations in force, with 5 percent (23,118) realized during the spring campaign. Although children are included in the 23,118, a significant number were registered by their parents or guardians as the adults registered for cards themselves. The strategic planning by staff and the positive reception of the registration campaigns by the public put the library well ahead of its projection in meeting the "500,000 in 2000" goal.

Representatives of five of the companies that hosted drives called the library to arrange a repeat effort in the fall. One called several times to remind the library that they wanted librarians to set up a registration drive when the new Independence Branch Library was to open a block away from their headquarters. Library employees from many job classifications volunteered to participate in the drives, which engendered a sense of investment in the outcome. Staff saw each other as equal members of the team when they were together in the heat of a flea market or the cold of a transit station entrance.

PHASE 3—FALL 2000

A focus group of children's and adult/young adult librarians was convened in the spring to identify target audiences and materials for the fall student campaign. The focus group felt that kindergartners and seventh graders were the most important groups to reach—one group as they are starting school and one as they become "young adults" and are eligible for an adult card.

After reviewing the materials from the previous two phases, the group liked the "big" library card (good for making class visits), the FLP banner, the poster advertising the library card registration, and the "house of worship" brochure (because it was simpler in design and layout). They liked the badges, but recommended, however, that future badges be clip-ons to avoid damage to clothing. They felt the kindergarten campaign was more effective than sending the brochures to the students' homes. They also said they would be willing to go to the schools and pick up the kindergarten applications and said that the personal touch—of visiting classes—was vital to the success of the campaign.

Stephanie Childs of the Office of Kindergarten Support again requested 16,000 applications for the public school kindergarten teachers to share with the parents at the opening school conferences. Because of its popularity, the teddy bear design was incorporated into the special application form and some changes were made in the wording on the application. The FLP volunteer office recruited several volunteers to assemble the applications into packs of 30, and then package the exact number of packs needed for the kindergarten classrooms in each school. At Childs's recommendation, each packet was stamped with "TIME SENSITIVE MATERIAL—DO NOT DELAY" to expedite the delivery of the packets to the kindergarten teachers. Another change was that the branch children's librarian would call the school and make arrangements to pick up the completed applications. Again, children's librarians requested additional copies of the teddy bear applications to take to private and parochial kindergartens. The volunteer office filled all these requests.

The Philadelphia Coca-Cola Bottling Co. again donated 15,000 coupons (for a free bottle of Nestea) for the teen phase of the campaign. They also donated large banners to be used at schools and other registration drives. In addition, they donated on-air radio time and $3,600, which was used for promotional materials. AWE again donated a laptop computer to be given to a seventh grader who signed up for a card. A simple bookmark with a library card application and a list of branches was prepared for the seventh-grade registration drive and to highlight the contest. The School District of Philadelphia was in favor of the campaign but wanted letters to be sent to the parents first if school personnel were to hand them out. Because this requirement would have meant printing 13,000 letters, it was decided the librarians and teen outreach specialists would take them to the classrooms of the public, charter, private, and parochial schools. The winner was chosen at random by computer and was drawn from those students who had used their card in the last six months and had no overdue materials.

Stephanie Childs was a guest speaker at the reopening celebration of the West Oak Lane Branch Library and she gave an enthusiastic speech about the kindergarten campaign and about how important libraries are in the lives of children. "Carry the Card!" pencils were purchased for giveaways at registrations. Many branches that served as polling sites for the election had tables set up for library card registration. Librarians and the teen outreach specialists reported that their visits to seventh-grade classes often resulted in other benefits—booktalking new YA books, talking about teen summer reading programs, and showing school librarians and teachers about the many resources available through the FLP Web site.

By the end of the third phase of the library card campaign, the library had far exceeded its goal of 500,000. Staff took pride in their success; many staff broadened their horizons as to venues for registration outside of the four walls of the library. More schools began calling the branch libraries to arrange for librarians to visit. The library's visibility was dramatically increased through the publicity associated with the campaign (such as when Elliot Shelkrot, the president and director of the Free Library, was interviewed on several radio stations about the campaign). Not only did more people in the community learn about the library, the library learned about itself and how to improve its services. The library learned that despite best efforts, there will always be teachers who will not want class visits and parents who refuse to give permission for their children to register. The library also increased the opportunity for staff input in the later phases. Focus groups were held and there were several e-mail surveys. Accepting staff input empowered them to create their own opportunities. But mostly the library learned the importance of targeting both its message and its audience. By attempting to appeal to every student in every grade in every school during Phase One, the library actually diffused the efforts rather than making a large impact. By Phase Three, the library focused its efforts on key grades, and in doing so achieved a higher return on its investment.

5 JOINING HANDS IN THE CITY OF BIG SHOULDERS: THE CHICAGO PUBLIC LIBRARY AND CHICAGO PUBLIC SCHOOLS' COOPERATIVE LIBRARY CARD CAMPAIGN

Kicking off its fourth year during the 2000–2001 school year, the library card campaign in Chicago is one of the most successful in the nation, in part because of the strong relationship with the Chicago Public Schools. The school system, through its department of libraries and information services, spearheads the annual campaign in the fall for every student who does not have one to get a public library card. Over 45,000 cards were issued during the 1999–2000 school year campaign. Impressive? Yes, but that has not even been the best year of the campaign. In 1998 over 60,000 students signed up for library cards. This was an increase of 43 percent over the first year of the campaign. The most recent campaign, for the year 2000–2001 academic year, netted almost 55,000 registrations.

The program for the year 2000–2001 school year began with school librarians receiving a packet of informational materials from the Chicago Public Library as part of a workshop in August. The packet included sample forms, instructions, a map of the library system, and a list of branch contacts. For school librarians unable to attend the meeting, the packet was mailed or delivered to the school. The library card application is more than just another form to fill out, but rather it is an attractive promotional document reprinted in a variety of colors with instructions and information for parents and students printed on the back. The campaign has firm deadlines, requiring every school to deliver completed applications to their neighborhood branch library by the end of September. In many branches, library staff traveled to schools to pick up materials. At each branch library one person was assigned as the contact person for the library card campaign. In most cases, the person assigned to this task was the branch children's librarian. During the month of October, library staff processed the cards so they were ready for pick-up by November 1. The library's circulation coordinator, working with clerical staff in each branch cluster, helps manage the workload among locations. By December 1, the library and the school district can announce schools that have the highest percentage of students with library cards. Although aimed at grades 1–12 of the Chicago Public Schools, private and parochial schools, as well as kindergarten and pre-K classes, are invited to participate.

Those public schools with over 75 percent of their students holding library cards are given special recognition (often in the form of grants to build the library collection) by the Chicago Public Schools' Department of Library and Information Services. The "library card honor roll" has three levels:

- Gold (95 percent registered)
- Silver (75 percent registered)
- Platinum (95 percent maintained for two years)

It is the responsibility of the schools to verify the registration numbers using forms provided by the library. In addition, it is the role of the teacher to verify the information on the application. The school is also responsible for contacting the branch library, picking up sufficient library card applications (available in English, Spanish, and Polish), and returning the applications to the branch, as well as all necessary forms. Those students who do not have a card, or who have lost their cards, are given an application. Each teacher in each school handled the process differently, but generally, teachers would review with their students the importance of having a card, the instructions for filling out the form, and the process for returning the completed application. Since the school would receive incentives for meeting certain goals, many teachers and school librarians would not only tell the students about these rewards, but would also develop small incentives of their own to motivate students to return the forms.

The school and the library work together once the applications have been processed and the cards are ready for pick-up. For problems with fines and for lost or unreturned books, the library developed a form to send back to the student. During the campaign, students may get a new library card for free as the replacement card fee is waived. Yet, the library has found that schools often need a phone call, e-mail, or visit to remind them. According to the library administration, the success of the campaign over the past few years has been, in large part, because staff actively made first contact with the schools in the area.

Within the schools, school librarians are the leaders and over the years they have developed a wide variety of innovative ideas to promote library card sign-ups, such as:

- Displaying an oversized copy of the Chicago Public Library card on a bulletin board and surrounding it with a strand or two of flashing holiday lights, or challenging the students to create a unique border design (such as names of libraries they have visited or activities they've participated in at their branch library).
- Honoring the class that achieves 100 percent registration first with a pizza party or some other rewards.
- Sponsoring a parade through the halls with students waving their library cards.
- Asking students to create commercials (posters, audio, or video) urging their fellow students to register for library cards.
- Creating an "Honor Roll Chart" for the library bulletin board by listing the names of students that have library cards under their homeroom or class number.
- Presenting certificates of achievement to classes that achieve a specific percentage and asking students to display these certificates outside their classrooms so fellow students, teachers, and visitors can see them.
- Taking and displaying photographs of classes holding their library cards.
- Sponsoring a craft activity where the students create a wallet for their library cards by folding, stapling together, and then decorating interesting paper (such as wallpaper, file folders, or heavy construction paper).
- Creating a "Show Your Library Card Day," including a rally with cheers, songs, and skits that salute libraries and reading.
- Passing out candy, bookmarks, stickers, or other small incentives to students who get or already have library cards.

In addition to these activities planned by school librarians, individual classroom teachers have shown tremendous initiative and innovation motivating their students to complete the application and get a library card. One element of success was a library card campaign rap, which was used by teachers, school librarians, and public librarians during their visits.

Support from the library card program runs from the classroom teacher all the way up to the mayor of Chicago, Richard M. Daley, who noted that "the education of all Chicago's children is vitally important. Good schools and good libraries go hand in hand. A library card is a free pass to lifelong learning. It is the most important school supply that a child can possess." Support for the library card campaign, like that of Mayor Lee P. Brown in Houston, was critical to Mayor Daley being honored as *Library Journal*'s "Politician of the Year."

See the **"Gallery of Successful Library Card Campaign Programs" for these documents from the Chicago Public Library:**

√ Library Card Rap
√ Receipt for Library Cards
√ Form for Incomplete or Unsuccessful Application

PUTTING ON THE GLITZ: THE LOS ANGELES PUBLIC LIBRARY'S LIBRARY CARD CAMPAIGN

When is a library card campaign not a library card campaign? When it is so much more. With eye-catching billboards, slick promotional material, and a wide range of celebrities lined up in support, the Los Angeles Public Library launched a library card campaign in the summer of 1988 that transformed into a broader-based promotional effort to enhance the image of the library in community. In addition, the campaign strove to increase the traffic coming into the Central Library and the branch libraries. While the tangible part of the campaign was to increase registration and use, the intangible aspects, such as increasing community visibility and increasing staff morale, were just as important.

The campaign was actually conducted by the Library Foundation of Los Angeles, the fund-raising arm of the library. To implement the library card sign-up drive, the Library Foundation hired a marketing firm to design the campaign. The campaign would use all media and reach throughout Los Angeles to all demographic group, with particular attention paid to the target audiences of adults age 18–49, who represent a large portion of the city's population. This key demographic group, compared to seniors and school-age children, was underrepresented in terms of having a library card. An advertising and design firm was subcontracted to develop materials, slogans, and a graphic approach to reaching the target market. The foundation developed a task force to interact with the marketing firm and approve its plans. The task force asked for the plan, which called for paid media, to be modified. The task force members, representing major corporations, began working with the marketing firm in developing sponsorships to support the campaign based on cash or in-kind donations, rather than paid media spots.

Sponsors soon came on board, including the *Los Angeles Times,* United Airlines, the Los Angeles Philharmonic, and Eller Outdoor Media. Starting with those companies as a base, other corporations were approached with some of the pitches developed by three subcontracted ethnic market public relations firms. One major sponsor was the television station KNX. KNX produced public service announcements (PSAs) which were distributed through the station to the South California Association of Broadcasters in both radio and video form. The spots featured long-time supporters of the Los Angeles Public Library, as well as celebrities (including actors Gregory Peck, Jack Lemmon, and Bill Pullman, former LA Lakers star Kareem Abdul-Jabbar, and Mayor Richard J. Riordan) recruited for the campaign

The campaign rolled out under the banner of "Sign of Intelligent Life in LA: Get Your Free Library Card Today" on July 1, 1998, with a press conference at City Hall which featured the chair of the library foundation, the director of the library, the mayor, a city council member, and Kareem Abdul-Jabbar. The press conference was held against the backdrop of the campaign billboard featuring the slogan, art, and graphic approach. The press conference was covered by every major Los Angeles broadcast and print outlet, including a photo and story in the *Los Angeles Times*. A group of children from City Hall day care center was also in attendance to hear Mayor Riordan tell them, "Our children deserve to experience the magic of reading. . . . The campaign will help encourage children and adults all over Los Angeles to get a library card and visit their local library." The chairman of the Library Foundation stressed that having a card for the Los Angeles Public Library means "you're an Angeleno—you've got something in common with all residents of this fantastic, ethnically diverse city."

While the Library Foundation was the backbone of the campaign, other sponsors soon came on board to support the campaign. United Airlines sponsored library card nights at the Hollywood Bowl, featuring library and foundation volunteers (adorned in "Signs of Intelligent Life in LA" T-shirts) who signed up concertgoers for library cards. United Airlines donated prizes to be used as an incentive, and sponsored a sweepstakes offering a chance to win round-trip tickets to Washington, D.C., for signing up for a library card. Campaign counter cards and library card applications were placed in ticket offices of United Airlines all over the city. Pacific Bell sponsored library card night at Dodger Stadium. Folks who attended the game had the opportunity to sign up for a library card at three tables staffed by library staff and volunteers. In addition, the Kareem Abdul-Jabbar PSA was shown on the large scoreboard (Dodger Vision) and the PSA was read over the public address system.

The art, slogan, and graphics were shown on Pacific Theater movie screens at the chain's locations around the city. Moviegoers were encouraged to pick up a library card brochure/application which was easily accessible from a counter top display at the concession stand. The grocery store chain Ralph's/Food 4 Less underwrote the production of 150,000 of the brightly colored brochures. These brochures contained information about the library, a map, and a tear-off application; they were available in English and Spanish. Like the billboards, the brochures featured the key slogans, art, and graphic design. The colors of yellow, green, purple, and orange were primarily used on the brochure, as well as on a redesigned library card.

The bright color scheme was meant not merely to attract attention to the new library card and campaign surrounding it, but also to give the library a more "contemporary" look. The counter displays, posters, and other materials produced for the campaign all stuck to the same color scheme and graphic design. At the press conference announcing the campaign, Library Director Susan Kent hit on this theme, noting "people who haven't been to a Los Angeles Public Library lately may be surprised when they visit." A residual of the campaign, according to Peter Persic, the library's public information director, was that it provided the library with an "exciting, new identity and new hip look." In doing so, it created excitement among not only new library users, but also the staff of the library. Using the slogan "Books are only the beginning," the campaign was as much about shaking up the public stereotypes of libraries and changing the library's image as it was about getting more people to get cards and use the library.

The 1998 campaign was actually the second large library card campaign undertaken by the Los Angeles Public Library during the decade. In 1991 the library teamed with the Los Angeles Unified School District, as well as private and parochial schools, to launch the "Library Card for Every Child" campaign. During the sign-up drive, which kicked off with a press conference featuring Mayor Tom Bradley reading a proclamation about the campaign, librarians for Los Angeles Public Library attempted to visit, at least once, every school in the city. At each school, the library attempted to make brief presentations before every grade about the importance of getting a library card. Librarians then distributed a newly designed and simplified library card application. The application was printed in English and Spanish, while instruction sheets on filling out the application were also prepared in Armenian, Chinese, Farsi, Korean, Russian, and Vietnamese. Students were asked to take the applications home, have them filled out, and then return them to school. School personnel returned the applications to the library. Staff processed the cards, and then mailed them to the students' homes.

In large cities like Los Angeles, Chicago, Philadelphia, and

Houston, all of which feature large recent-immigrant populations as well as highly mobile citizens, library card campaigns need to be under constant consideration. Not only does a new campaign every decade bring in all of the newcomers to the city, but it can also serve to reenergize staff. One of the primary benefits, according to the administration of the Los Angeles Public Library, was again not the impact of the library card campaign on the public, but the impact on the staff of the library. For many members of the Los Angeles Public Library staff, the campaign gave them a feeling of pride that they were doing something important and that their work had value.

See the "Gallery of Successful Library Card Campaign Programs" for this document from the Los Angeles Public Library

√   Sign of Intelligent Life in LA Brochure/Application

7 GOING WILD ABOUT READING: THE LIBRARY CARD CAMPAIGN OF THE SAN JOSE PUBLIC LIBRARY

During his state of the city address in 1999, San Jose Mayor Ron Gonzales announced his desire to get library cards in the hands of every first and second grader in San Jose. On the very next day, the staff of the San Jose Public Library began planning a pilot program. One of the library branches was closing for a month for renovation, so it was decided to use that staff to implement the pilot with one of the 16 school districts served by the library. A pilot program would allow the library to "test the waters" of such a large undertaking and develop important relationships with school personnel, but primarily the library would be able to develop processes and procedures that could be utilized for a larger campaign.

The library created special library card applications for the project. Working closely with the school district's director of student services (who was a member of the library's planning team), a plan was developed to distribute applications and establish a schedule of class visits. Applications were returned to the library and cards were created. Children's librarians visited the classrooms individually, gave a presentation on the library and its services, and handed out library cards. As a special bonus for these children, the library received a sponsorship from Pacific Bell that allowed the library to give every child in the class (including those who already had or didn't want cards) canvas book bags. Pacific Bell also gave the library the money to purchase hardback books to give to the classroom teachers who helped make the program happen.

While the pilot was extremely labor-intensive, it was also very successful, with over 1,300 new library cards issued. From the pilot, the library developed the "Wild About Reading" campaign (which kicked off in March 2000, with a press conference at the Biblioteca Latinoamerica) to put library cards in the hands of the other 23,000 first and second graders served by the San Jose Public

Library by May 2001. At the press conference Mayor Gonzales noted, "For our community to be successful, we must work together as a community to ensure that all San Jose children can read by the third grade. Public librarians in partnership with our schools will help our youngest students discover the excitement of reading and encourage them to explore the worlds contained on library shelves." Pacific Bell was on hand as well, handing over a check for $25,000 to support the program. A spokesperson for the company noted that "Pacific Bell recognizes the critical need to improve the reading skills for all San Jose school children, Silicon Valley's next generation of workers and leaders. We believe this program will help our community see our libraries as exciting places to both learn and have fun."

The program provided a cooperative project to strengthen the links between the public and the public schools, in particular the San Jose public schools. The "Wild About Reading" campaign dovetailed nicely into the district's focus on improving literacy. Other partners who were necessary to the success of the program were parents. This viewpoint was noted in an editorial in the *San Jose Mercury News* on the Sunday following the kickoff. The editorial noted, "We wish each library card application could include the explicit statement that parents' participation is non-negotiable."

To reach the mayor's goal, the library divided the city districts into "chunks" so that individual branches would concentrate their efforts during just a single semester. In a procedure similar to that for the pilot, the librarian would visit classrooms according to a schedule coordinated by "Wild About Reading" liaisons in the school district office. During the visit, the librarian would display and discuss library materials, share the joy of reading through storytelling, and distribute library card applications to all the students. The staff would also provide the teacher with an evaluation and a reporting form, as well as a self-addressed envelope for returning the application. The reporting form, modeled after the one created by the Phoenix Public Library, provided incentives for teachers to return the applications. For just returning the application, a teacher would receive a free book for the classroom, but for returning applications for every student in the class, the teacher's name was entered into a drawing to win 1 of 25 gift certificates to a local bookstore worth $100.

An important element to enlist the support of schools was asking each school district to adopt a formal resolution supporting the "Wild About Reading" program. In addition, each branch library was assigned a contact person within the school district to help schedule classroom visits and meetings with principals.

By the spring of 2001 the library met the goal of having offered every first and second grader in San Jose the opportunity to get a library card. By April 2001 the library had visited 14,123 kids in 873 classes in 101 schools and issued 6,187 new cards.

Mayor Gonzales has been so pleased with the results of the project that he wants it to become an ongoing program. The library is thus looking at methods to make it less labor-intensive for the library and for the schools. One method toward improving the program was to ask classroom teachers to complete a survey at the end of each visit. In addition to providing the library with lots of good information about the program and enabling the library to function more efficiently, the survey was also used to recruit teachers to serve as an advisory council for the program. The library was successful in recruiting teachers by offering them each a $100 gift certificate for attending three meetings to provide the library with advice and guidance.

Planning for the campaign in fall 2001 involves hosting a kickoff event at a nice venue such as a hotel. The library will invite first-grade teachers and principals to attend. At the event, the educators will have plenty of food to eat while learning about the revised program. Those in attendance at the kickoff event will then act as ambassadors for the program in their schools, spreading the word and spearheading the program. Children's librarians will arrange to provide an assembly-style presentation to the entire school. Teachers will be given packets of applications and letters to distribute to parents. Once they collect completed student applications, the teachers will mail them back to the library. The library will provide incentives for teachers to participate and additional incentives for 100 percent return of applications. Upon receiving the applications, library staff will prepare the cards and mail them back to the teachers with letters to the parents. The library will then provide incentives for the parents to visit the library with their children.

The program has not been without drawbacks, the most noticeable being the need to cancel regular story times, special programs, and other children's events because staff was scheduled to be in the schools rather than in the branch library. The San Jose experience does bring up a central contradiction of most library card campaigns. To be successful, the campaigns need to include outreach to schools to motivate staff and students to get cards and use the library. Yet, these new users may find that staff is not available or programs are not offered or collections are not weeded, because staff members have been so busy with outreach that they have been unable to maintain their traditional work. Indeed, a successful campaign will increase traffic and circulation, but an increase in staffing or other resources are not always required to serve new customers. What is needed, in many cases, is staff hired or reassigned specifically to make the campaign their number one priority. Such was the case in Houston with staff hired just for the campaign, while in Portland, Oregon, the campaign became a project of staff hired just to do outreach with the schools.

See the "Gallery of Successful Library Campaign Programs" for these documents from the San Jose Public Library:

√ Wild About Reading Application Return Form
√ Wild About Reading Application

8 THE GREAT LIBRARY CARD ADVENTURE AND GET CARDED!: THE LIBRARY CARD CAMPAIGNS FOR STUDENTS, FACULTY, AND STAFF FROM THE MULTNOMAH COUNTY PUBLIC LIBRARY IN PORTLAND, OREGON

Focusing on the needs of school students became a top priority at the Multnomah County Library, which serves the city of Portland, Oregon, and the surrounding area. Rather than complaining about school cooperation, or the lack thereof, the library took a bold step to do something about it. It is not so much that libraries serve schools, but they do serve students, and the best place to find students together, and therefore deliver efficient and effective services, is in their schools. Thus, the library made a commitment to develop the "School Corps" team which would act as the primary contacts with schools. This small group of librarians works successfully with schools on a wide variety of projects, taking school and public library cooperation to a higher level than seen in most library systems.

The first major School Corps initiative was to make sure that every school-age child had a library card, which would involve not only a campaign to get new sign-ups, but also a method to document the number of students in each school who were already cardholders. But success breeds success, and one program was followed by another and then by three more; by summer of 2001 the library had conducted five separate library card campaigns, all captained by Jackie Partch, the Multnomah County Library School Corps team leader.

During the first campaign in the 1997–1998 school year, the library conducted the Great Library Card Adventure campaign for students in grades K–5 and the Get Carded! campaign aimed at students in grades 6–12. While similar in some ways, the campaigns were marked by different graphics, color schemes, slogans, and incentives for participation. The first year, the library issued 11,000 library cards. These campaigns, with slight modifications, were scheduled to be repeated in the 2001–2002 school year. In addition, the library extended the Great Library Card Adventure campaign to kindergarten students, which has resulted in over 1,500 new library cards each school year.

The first Great Library Card Adventure began in the fall of 1997 and it was the first major project of the School Corps. While many schools had some experience working with the library, this program provided a high-profile project to demonstrate to principals, teachers, and school library media specialists the value of cooperating with the public library. The goal of the School Corps is to increase the information literacy of faculty and students in the county through partnership. The letter sent to school personnel about the library card campaign also contained an informational brochure describing the School Corps and the other opportunities for school/public library partner projects.

The library also partnered with Starbucks, the national coffee company, to produce the program. Starbucks has a long history of supporting literacy and therefore was a perfect partner. In return for Starbucks' support, the library offered the company high visibility, including their name/logo on all the documents that went to schools and mentioning Starbucks in press releases and other library public information documents. Since one key to a successful library card campaign is getting teachers on board, Starbucks was asked to donate over 2,000 free drink coupons for every teacher who sent in a packet of student applications. But the major Starbucks funding was to support performances of the children's play *Green Eggs and Ham and Gertrude McFuzz* by the Northwest Children's Theater. A performance of the play went to the five schools that recorded the highest percentage of students, faculty, and staff who signed up for library cards. In addition, the school with the highest number of sign-ups not only got a performance of the play, but also ten new hardcover books for the media center. While most of the focus was on providing teachers with incentives to participate in the program and get students signed up, students who applied for new cards or already had cards received a Great Library Card Adventure sticker.

Letters to principals and media specialists went out in mid September. Attached to the letter was a preaddressed and prestamped postcard for each school to return to the library requesting a Great Library Card Adventure kit. The kit contained instructions for teachers, posters, as well as the requested number of library card applications. School Corps staff provided schools with the kits and acted as the main contact point. Teachers were instructed to mail their applications back to the School Corps office for processing. If applications were, however, dropped at branch libraries, branch staff forwarded them on to the School Corps. This ensured that all processing of applications were handed centrally. If staff found that a student already was registered for a library card, the old card was set to "lost" and the student was told to contact the nearest branch library. The same procedure was also followed if a student had incurred fines or lost book charges on a previous card. Cards without problems were returned to the teachers to distribute to their students.

The School Corps invited 150 schools to participate during the first year. Over two-thirds of the schools (103) returned the postcard and received a kit. Only a few schools then failed to follow up and send in applications, which resulted in a total of 90 schools actively participating. These schools represented eight separate school districts, as well as a large number of private schools. In addition, the NE Home Schoolers Association joined in the campaign. Four schools tied for first place by getting 100 percent of students, faculty, and staff—two were suburban school districts, one was from the Portland School District, and one was a private school. A private school was the fifth winning school, falling just short with a 99.44 percent sign-up rate. Although not every school ended the program with everyone having cards, every school district showed dramatic increases. Only 21 percent of students, faculty, and staff had cards at the beginning of the program, but that figure had more than doubled (to 47 percent) by the end of the program. Most dramatic was the increase in the Portland School District, the largest of all the districts. Less than 20 percent of students, faculty, and staff reported having library cards before the program began. By November of the first year, however, the rate had increased to 47 percent reporting having library cards. The Great Library Card Adventure spiked library card registration numbers, resulting in a 29 percent increase over the previous year.

Building on the success of the Great Library Card Adventure, School Corps launched in January the Get Carded! campaign aimed at middle and high school students. The focus of this campaign was directly on the students rather than on teachers. The key aspect of the project was the creation of the KewlCard which was issued to every student (as well as faculty and staff) who applied for a card or already had a library card. The KewlCard added value to the library card by offering students discounts at a wide variety of merchants, including:

- Barnes and Noble
- B. Dalton
- Bike Gallery
- Noah's Bagel
- Powell's Books (a world famous local bookstore)
- Tower Books
- Tower Records
- Waldenbooks

A total of 14 vendors participated and had their logos printed on the Get Carded! promotional materials. The KewlCard could be used at the merchants during the month of April.

In many ways, the two campaigns were similar. In the Get Carded! campaign the letters to schools contained a postcard to request kits. Kits were sent, applications were returned with a tally sheet noting the number of students with cards and the number applying, and the cards were issued by the teachers. In addition to distributing the library cards, teachers handed out the KewlCards. They also handed out a great number of library cards, with five schools (two suburban schools and three private schools) all reporting 100 percent registration. Again, the results were dramatic. Before the program, only 15 percent of students, faculty, and staff at area middle and high schools had cards; after the program, the number stood at 50 percent.

After campaigning in the higher grades successfully, the School Corps aimed to get all kindergartners registered for cards in the fall of 2000. The Great Library Card Adventure for kindergartners resembled the program for elementary students with just a few variations. There was a different sponsor (Diedrich Coffee) for teacher incentives and a different program (a professional juggler) with slightly different criteria. The competition for the prize was not just among schools, but also among kindergarten classes. Each class that achieved 100 percent sign-ups had its name put in a drawing to win one of five visits by the juggler. In total, 37 classrooms achieved the goal; they all received a $10 gift certificate to the library's Tidal Wave bookstore, or a same priced certificate to Powell Books. Three of the five classrooms winning the drawing came from the Portland Schools, with one from a suburban school, and the other from a private school.

The kindergarten program added another 1,300 library cards issued. Before the Great Library Adventure, only 15 percent of kindergarten students, faculty, and staff in the participating schools had library cards. That number more than doubled due to the program, which resulted in almost 55 percent of students in those schools calling themselves cardholders.

The Multnomah County Library card campaign achieved its goal of increasing the number of children with library cards, but just as important, the campaign also served as a project to kick-start the School Corps project. The planning process began by reviewing the library's previous library card campaign (which was long past) as well as querying other libraries about their successful campaigns. Planning for Get Carded! involved working with the county's youth advisory board about publicity and incentives. (For example, the teens suggested using individual incentives rather than the schoolwide incentives used for the younger kids.) While there was publicity regarding the campaign in the community, the bulk of the campaign was really through the school. The school media specialist was the primary contact at each school. The media specialists distributed the materials to teachers and collected all the applications to send back to the School Corps. One media specialist and one principal wanted so badly to get 100 percent participation at their school that they actually made home visits to get applications to the last few students without cards. In middle and high schools, this arrangement was often more flexible, since these media specialists often didn't see the students on a regular basis. Some schools even had students volunteer to sign up other students at lunchtime.

Getting others to assist was necessary since the four School Corps members conducted the entire campaign for over 250 schools. Although it was impossible for staff to visit each school personally during the campaign, they did promote library card registration when they were at schools providing other services, such as information literacy instruction and booktalking. While the visits certainly stoked enthusiasm for the program, two of the strongest parts of the Multnomah County Library program were the popular incentives (the coffee coupons and KewlCards especially) and the flexibility of the program, which allowed each school to run the program in a way that worked for them. The only requirement was that the applications be returned by a certain date with the "tally sheet" which showed the total number of student in the class, the number applying for cards, and the number who already had cards. By making it easier for teachers to participate and by motivating them to do so, students were the real winners.

See the "Gallery of Successful Library Card Campaign Programs" for these documents from the Multnomah County Public Library:

√ Get Carded! Poster
√ Great Library Card Adventure Poster
√ Great Library Card Adventure Instructions for Teachers
√ Get Carded! Instruction for Teachers
√ Great Library Card Adventure Postcard for Kindergarten
√ Great Library Card Adventure Kit Information

A STAR CARD IN THE LONE STAR STATE: THE LIBRARY CARD CAMPAIGN OF THE AUSTIN PUBLIC LIBRARY

The Austin Public Library's Star Card campaign began with a simple question: why don't more kids have library cards? The impetus for the program came from many factors, but one important element was information culled from several citywide library focus group sessions. At these sessions, concern was expressed about the ways to remove barriers that prevent youth from applying for library cards and utilizing the library. The concern developed into a library project to inform Austin area youth about library services—especially nonusers, many of whom are non–English-speaking youths in low-income areas. The library also had anecdotal information from staff, which indicated that many parents would not let their children have a library card because they were afraid they couldn't pay the fines. Finally, the library also had statistical information that clearly showed the library facilities in low-income areas were underutilized. Certainly an underserved market was waiting to be tapped.

The library created a task force in the spring 1999 to prepare and roll out the Star Card campaign in the fall during National Children's Book Week. The task force, with representatives from locations in all parts of the city and all levels of seniority, was comprised of branch managers, assistant branch managers, youth services staff members, circulation support staff members, and individuals from library administration. The circulation manager for the library was named to chair the task force. The team met throughout the summer and until the kickoff in November. The task force brainstormed ideas and then was empowered to act on them (such as renaming the library card for kids the "Star Card"). Working with library administration, the task force set two primary goals:

- To provide the opportunity for every young person in the greater Austin area to obtain a youth card free of charge.

- To augment the youth materials collection with the addition of $250,000 the first year.

The goals go together: the first goal aimed to increase the number of youth users by offering them, through their schools, a chance to get a card, and the second goal aimed to make sure there were sufficient materials at the library when students came in to put those new cards to use.

One of the early decisions of the library's task force was to work closely with the Austin Public Schools, as both institutions are concerned with youth literacy. A pilot collaborative effort between one Austin Independent School District school (Sanchez Elementary) and one Austin Public Library location (the Terrazas Branch Library) was successfully completed during the spring 1999 semester. Thanks to the efforts of Branch Manager Elva Garza and Principal Ed Leo, over 50 percent of the students received their own library card, and over 85 percent of these cards were used in the first three months. Based on the success of this pilot project, Austin Public Library (APL) decided to forge ahead with a large campaign and initiate a new special card just for kids.

Early in the planning stages for the new youth card, APL staff realized that more Austin area youth could be reached and greater participation from parents could be achieved by working directly with the local schools. Representing the APL Star Card task force, Nancy Toomhs approached AISD about partnering with the library in an effort to get library cards into the hands of the children of the Austin area—by opening the Star Card program to all students at all schools. This partnership was enthusiastically received, and it has been mutually beneficial.

The AISD administrative supervisor for library services became the library's lead contact person. She distributed a letter of support to all school principals, hosted Austin Public Library attendance at librarians' meetings, and provided excellent input on the best approach for the project. The school librarians were usually the first contact person in the schools. They helped the library schedule visits to classrooms and staff meetings, and they distributed and gathered materials from teachers and students.

Generous assistance from the community allowed APL to widely publicize the creation and implementation of the new Star Card. During the summer of 1999 the Austin Public Library Foundation conducted a community-wide contest for children to design the new Star Card. Entry forms were distributed at story times and summer reading program events, and at more than 20 area HEB grocery stores. The *Austin American-Statesman* made the entry forms available by fax through their "Inside Line" service and donated advertising space to publicize the contest. A panel of volunteer judges selected top entries for each of three age categories from more than 300 entries, and then they selected the winning design. Lucia Jazayeri, a 12-year-old student at AISD's Murchison Middle School submitted the winning entry, a graphically powerful expression of the diversity of the Austin community. The design of the Star Card was an opportunity to involve local youth in the Star Card's creation while raising public interest in the new card.

The children's entries were exhibited at Highland Mall in July 1999 and a press conference was held to unveil the new Star Card. The winning entry was also introduced at an Austin City Council meeting, and the artist was honored at a meeting of the AISD board of trustees. On November 13, 1999, at a press conference at the Old Quarry Branch Library, Lucia Jazayeri was the first young person to use a Star Card. HEB continued its support by providing prizes for the finalists, and the Friends of the Austin Public Library provided T-shirts featuring the winning design for all library staff. The T-shirts were also printed for sale to the public by the Austin Public Library Foundation. A local architectural firm donated services to create a portable exhibit of the entries and the winning design; the exhibit was then displayed at the Texas Book Festival, November 5–7, 1999, at the Texas State Capitol, and at the Austin Children's Museum, November 15–December 20, 1999.

To make the Star Card promotion a success, it was vital to partner with AISD, the largest school district served by the library. A resolution was passed by the AISD board of trustees recognizing the AISD student whose drawing was selected as the winning entry for the Star Card art and recognizing the staff of APL for its effort to "promote literacy among students of AISD." AISD supported the kickoff of the new Star Card by supplying posters to all AISD campuses promoting the new library card. Other support included the collection of overdue APL materials at school libraries during "Clean Slate for Kids" in November 1999, and the provision of drop boxes in each school library for "lost and found" APL materials.

APL Star Card task force members visited the AISD librarian's district meetings to talk about the Star Card and the partnership with the schools. The task force also attended a meeting of the Austin Council of Parent Teacher Associations to request their help and support in the Star Card project in the schools. Library staff members further promoted the APL Star Card by wearing Star Card T-shirts to all their outreach activities. They also took a poster-size version of the Star Card when attending school programs, literacy fairs, and community events.

During the spring 2000 semester, APL staff took Star Card applications to each of the 73 elementary schools in the Austin Independent School District. Teachers sent applications home with students and returned completed forms to APL. Approximately two weeks after receiving the completed forms, library staff took Star Cards to the schools for teachers to distribute to their students. This process provided over 44,000 elementary-age children an opportunity to obtain a Star Card. Following completion of the campaign in elementary schools during the fall 2000 and spring 2001 semesters, the library expanded school visits to include secondary schools. Visits to senior high schools are planned for the fall of 2001.

Because of the heavy workload and numerous competing demands for the attention of both students and teachers within the schools, it was necessary for the library to create interest about the program in the community at large. In part, the purpose of this new approach is to energize parents and/or have them ask their children about their Star Card applications. In addition, its purpose is to let the community know that the library is not interested in only youth literacy issues, but also actively involved in a campaign to increase reading. To this end, the library developed media advisories, public service announcements, news releases, letters to talk show producers, as well as using personal contact with reporters and editors. These efforts paid off big time with coverage of the campaign by television, radio, and print (both the large daily and community papers). A proclamation by the Austin City Council, covered by the city's live government channel, was broadcast and then rebroadcast to provide further public exposure. Austin City Connection, the City of Austin's Web site, promoted the program and provided links to the Austin Public Library site. A story announcing the Star Card also was on the front page of *At Your Doorstep,* a monthly publication produced by the City of Austin's Public Information Office and mailed to more than 450 registered neighborhood associations and about 100 others who have requested it. Finally, to communicate information about library services and the Star Card to a larger audience, the library also increased bilingual signage and printed materials.

To support the campaign, the library prepared a large number and variety of public relations materials. Some were planned strategically for distribution in the various library locations, others for distribution specifically through the AISD/school outreach project, and still others as follow-up materials mailed to new cardholders. There was a press conference to announce the winner of the card design contest, and another held when the first card was issued to the design contest winner at her local branch. Both were attended by city dignitaries. Several early morning radio talk show sessions were aired during the initial implementation of the new Star Card and "Clean Slate for Kids" week, and an APL-produced video was broadcast over two local television stations and videotaped for viewing throughout the schools.

Additionally, the library staff attended many community events throughout the year, such as the annual "Teddy Bear Picnic," "Coats for Kids," and various city cultural festivals, and issued Star Cards on the spot. On average, the library participated in two to three events per month. Twice, library staff participated as volunteers on the "phone banks" during the local PBS affiliate's fund drive, the second time offering over the air to sign youth up for Star Cards during the pledge breaks. This initiative, held during early Saturday morning programming, resulted in more new youth cardholders.

But while lots of things were going on in public, some of the key elements of the program involved administrative decisions to remove barriers to youth getting library cards. To make the program succeed, the library changed its requirements to obtain a library card so that students could register through the schools, rather than needing to register in a library with an adult present. To encourage sign-ups—and, even more, to encourage older children who no longer used their cards due to excessive fines—the Star Card was kicked off with "Clean Slate for Kids" during National Children's Book Week, allowing youth to clear their records when they registered for the Star Card. Further, the library reduced fines on youth materials from 20 cents per day per item to 5 cents per day per item. Working with city council and the mayor, the library eliminated a fee for nonresident youth, so that all students in the greater Austin area could obtain a Star Card. This change made extending the program to private and parochial schools much easier. Finally, the library created new bilingual English/Spanish registration materials as well as new "Just for Kids" brochures in Spanish and English, which highlight services and materials for youth and are distributed with the Star Card.

The Austin Public Library's Star Card initiative successfully completed its 1999 kickoff thanks to the partnership with AISD. By making application forms for each student available through the schools' distribution system, the library's services have been more accessible to students and their families—encouraging youth and their families to use the library and promoting literacy throughout the community. In the first three days (November 15–

17, 1999), 722 first-time cards were issued and 594 youth traded in their old cards—a total of 1,316 Star Cards. By the end of 1999 nearly 5,000 Star Cards had been issued. As of the end of February 2001, over 41,000 Star Cards have been issued.

See the "Gallery of Successful Library Card Campaign Programs" for these documents from the Austin Public Library:

√ Star Card Flyer
√ Star Card Application
√ Star Card "Dear Parent or Guardian" Letter

10 SUCCESS BREEDS SUCCESS: LIBRARY CARD CAMPAIGNS OF THE BIRMINGHAM PUBLIC LIBRARY AND THE JEFFERSON COUNTY LIBRARY COOPERATIVE

The work done by the Birmingham (Alabama) Public Library also represents a fantastic example of success breeding success. The library began with a library card campaign aimed at children, called Licensed to Read. It proved so successful that the library expanded the program to middle and high school students. That program, dubbed WILD Card, was built on the same model, but featured different graphics. The WILD Card proved so successful that a local sponsor (Pepsi) as well as a television station came aboard to expand the WILD Card to the entire metro area, thus involving the Jefferson County Library Cooperative. The cooperative had already been interested in library card campaigns, running an "Off to Great Start" campaign aimed at kindergarten and first graders to help celebrate the organization's 20th anniversary. The success of all these programs demanded that they become not one-shot deals, but instead ongoing campaigns to raise awareness of the library, to increase use, and to sign up more kids for library cards. The mission, however, is greater: to increase literacy. Created and run from the Birmingham Public Library's literacy branch, the Licensed to Read and WILD Card campaigns demonstrate what happens when good ideas prosper.

In the fall of 1998 the Birmingham Public Library entered into a pro-literacy partnership with the Birmingham Public Schools. The project, named Licensed to Read, was designed to help improve the reading skills of the city's students and will become a permanent part of the library's outreach program. The primary goals of Licensed to Read were to promote student literacy and

75

introduce the public library as a source for reading materials to all school students in Birmingham. The method to achieve the goals is to increase access to reading materials by increasing the number of students with public library cards. The specific objectives were to register all of Birmingham's students for library cards and instill in these young people the desire to use their cards. Research revealed that less than one-third of the city's youth were registered for library cards. The goal of the program was to increase that number to 90 percent. This ambitious project centered not just on creating awareness through a promotional campaign, but on developing an outreach campaign that would send representatives of the Birmingham Public Library to every school in the city.

The school visits included programs written especially for this project and delivered by members of the Birmingham Public Library staff and community volunteers. They are tailored for each audience and designed to showcase the multifaceted talents of library staff. The class visits lasted about 20 minutes and consisted of a book-based story time and a promotion for library cards and library use. For example, young audiences were delighted by a faux fairy tale involving a literate frog whose reply to every book recommendation is a bored, "read-it" response. The library then worked with each teacher individually to make sure the library application forms were sent home to parents.

The student registration process involved sending a specially designed library application home with each student to be filled out and signed by a parent or guardian. The library was responsible for picking up the completed library applications from the teacher and for getting the library cards to each child. If possible, the second visit to the classroom by a library staff member included promotion of reading and library use. The library requested that all parents fill out the application, even if their child already had a library card. After library staff had processed all the applications from a school, library staff visited the school. During this visit, each child received a special packet from the library. Packets for children who qualified for a library card contained the new card plus a game board for the Licensed to Read Scavenger Hunt. Children who already had valid library cards were not issued new cards, but they also received the Licensed to Read Scavenger Hunt game board. Parents of children whose application was not filled out fully and parents of children who had a charge on their current library card received notes asking them to go to their neighborhood library to clear up the problem. These children also received a Licensed to Read Scavenger Hunt game board. The Licensed to Read Scavenger Hunt was designed to be an easy and fun way for children to become familiar with the Birmingham Public Library. It can be completed in a short time and there is a reward for the young people who make the effort to get to know their library in this way.

The Licensed to Read project is a long-term project that targets school-age children in the City of Birmingham. The number of schools and classes in the city makes it impossible to visit each one in a single year. Therefore the project was planned to be implemented in three phases. During Phase One, implemented in the academic year 1998–1999, the library visited those Birmingham Public Schools with kindergarten through fifth grades. The following academic year, the plan was to visit the visit the remaining public schools in Phase Two. This includes the three city schools, which house grades kindergarten through eight. Phase Three targets the private school students within the City of Birmingham and was planned for 2000–2001. The campaign does not end with registration, but instead with a commitment to interact with students at key grades and to register new students. Visits are planned for students in kindergarten, sixth, and ninth grades. These are the grades that traditionally mark the beginning of new phases in the education process. The library wants to make sure that as each child makes a new beginning, he or she has that vital tool to school success: a library card.

A very important part of this project is the library/school partnerships. Each school in the City of Birmingham has been partnered with the branch of the Birmingham Public Library nearest the school. The public librarian will visit the school several times during the school year. Parents are also important partners in this effort. In the promotional material for the campaign, the library stressed the role of parents in helping their children enjoy reading. The library invited all parents in the city to join them and Birmingham Public Schools in making Licensed to Read an exciting and meaningful part of their children's education.

There were changes during the second year of the program. When the student returned the completed application to his or her teacher the student received a Licensed to Read sticker as an instant reward. Applications are then processed at the literacy branch of the Birmingham Public Library system. Every student returning an application is congratulated in writing for either receiving a new library card or already owning a library card. In addition, each is given a specially designed key chain that says, "Reading—I've Got the Key." These letters along with the new cards and key chains are returned to the school for distribution to the students. Each classroom that has a 50 percent or higher return rate of applications is rewarded with a Licensed to Read poster to hang in their classroom.

During the first year of the program, the library issued 4,460 new library cards to K–5 students in Birmingham Public Schools and confirmed that 2,636 students already had library cards. One immediate benefit of the Licensed to Read project was a 9 percent participant increase in the 1999 Library Summer Reading program. In addition, the library strengthened the lines of communication and collaboration between the Birmingham Public Library and the Birmingham Public Schools.

The program has been a success in meeting the library's goals of partnering public library branches with public schools, promoting student literacy, and introducing the public library as a source for reading materials. The development of stronger lines of communication and cooperation between the public library and the schools resulted and will be a lasting contribution of the program. Branch librarians now know whom to approach and how to gain entry to their partnered schools.

Still, the library found it a challenge to coordinate communication between the principal and school librarian to set up the initial discussion of the Licensed to Read program. To make the program work, the branch librarians were extremely flexible and able to make arrangements to be present at every scheduled meeting. For example, one staff member had tried for weeks to speak with a principal. She finally made contact one morning and was asked if someone from the library could come out to a meeting that very morning. Persistence was the key word in contacting principals.

The number of presentations of the Licensed to Read programs in each school was based on the enrollment figures and available space. In some schools the program was presented once to the entire student body in the gym. In other schools the program was presented twice—once for K–2 and then for grades 3–5. In one school, the library was able to present the program for each grade level. In the majority of schools, however, the program was presented in the gym as an assembly. Sometimes, if a gym was not available, the programs were held in school libraries, auditoriums, cafeterias, classrooms, and once inside a church across the street from the school.

The return rate of applications in the schools varied greatly. It ranged from a disappointing 11 percent at one school to an outstanding 96 percent at another school. Overall 45 percent of the library card applications were returned. There were several factors that contributed to the success of each school's campaign. The main factor was the enthusiasm of the principal and school librarian. The persistence on the part of the teacher in collecting the application form was also a contributing factor to the success of the Licensed to Read program.

After the actual processing of applications began, the library decided that several changes needed to be made in the process. First, simple, quick instructions for teachers needed to be included on the outside of each envelope containing applications. Second, the form given to students who already had a card or whose application was incomplete was unclear and it presented too many options for interpretation; that form was simplified. As the project progressed, the library also reevaluated the distribution of cards. In the beginning, it was decided that for an incomplete application, the available information would be added to the system without a barcode and a block placed on the record. A letter was then sent home with the child telling a parent to visit a library branch for more information. The same letter was also sent home with children who already had a card. This was confusing for parents, children, and librarians. Instead, with the new process the library card would be issued to a student even if the application was incomplete. A block would still be placed on the record and a note would be added to indicate the information needed to complete the application. The theory was that a child would be more likely to visit the library with a card in hand than with a piece of paper that could be interpreted in more than one way.

At the end of the program, the library sent to each of the school principals a thank-you letter and a report that included a chart with breakdowns of teachers and numbers/percentages of applications returned. Also included were figures of how many new cards were issued, how many students already had cards, and how many applications were incomplete. As school staff was the key to the success of the program, it was vital that they learn how well they were doing and how much their work was appreciated.

Principals were asked to be involved in the planning stages of the program. The associate director, literacy coordinator, and partnered public librarian attempted to meet with the principal and school librarian before the Licensed to Read project began in each school. This meeting normally lasted about a half hour. At the meeting, each principal was presented with a packet of general library information and was thoroughly briefed on the plans for the school visits. The library would then begin working with the school's contact person (the principal, or someone he or she had delegated) to schedule the visits. The school also supplied the library with a list of teachers and the number of students in each grade. Teachers were informed of the plans for the school visits through a library presentation at faculty meetings or personal letters mailed several weeks in advance.

The success of Licensed to Read led the library to focus on

students in upper grades, but it was recognized that the "cute" graphics wouldn't fly with secondary school students. Enter the WILD Card. During the 1999–2000 school year the Birmingham Public Library, in partnership with Birmingham Public Schools, initiated the WILD (Walking in Library Doors) Card project to target middle and high school students. This is an outreach project designed to promote the rich resources available to students and allow the students to complete a WILD Card application. The WILD Card is a regular library card with a WILD Card sticker affixed.

Each school is once again partnered with the nearest library branch. The staff from the partnered branch, along with staff members from the literacy branch, visit each school and present a program highlighting the library resources and the benefits available to students who own a library (WILD) card. After the initial year, the library will visit the schools each year targeting the sixth and ninth grades.

Specially designed library card applications, posters, and stickers have been created to generate interest and enthusiasm in the project and they are distributed to the students at the conclusion of the presentation. Applications are collected at the school and are then processed at the literacy branch of the Birmingham Public Library. Every student returning an application is congratulated in writing for either receiving a new library card or already owning a library card. In addition, each is given a WILD Card candy bar (a chocolate bar with a specially designed WILD Card wrapper). The candy bars have proven to be a wonderful incentive and reward for students.

In addition to visiting the middle and high schools, the library was asked to make presentations at two Birmingham Board of Education Adult Education Workplace sites, Guzzler Manufacturing and Miller Wire Works. In these visits the staff from the literacy branch presented an informal, often one-on-one, presentation of the public library and the resources available. Employees were encouraged to return the materials to the library branch nearest them and check out additional materials.

Due to the success of this literacy outreach project in Birmingham, television station WTTQ and the local Pepsi bottler wanted to see the program expand beyond the Birmingham Public Schools to the greater metro area. To make that happen, the Birmingham Public Library linked up with the Jefferson County Library Cooperative (of which Birmingham Public Library is a member) to extend the WILD Card program to all public libraries in the Birmingham metro area. Every library in the cooperative supported the program by having the WILD Card applications for students.

In August the television station began airing 30 promotional announcements they had produced to create excitement for the WILD Card program. The station ran the spots almost 300 times (15 times a week for 19 weeks). They also added their station logo to the WILD Card application and all promotional materials about the program. Pepsi kicked in by helping to fund many costs and offered a coupon for a free 20-ounce Pepsi for students completing the application. Libraries in the cooperative were instructed to process the applications like any other, but to issue the library card with a WILD Card sticker. Students already having a library card would get their cards "upgraded" with a WILD Card sticker.

See the "Gallery of Successful Library Card Campaign Programs" for these documents from the Birmingham Public Library and the Jefferson County Library Cooperative:

√ WILD Card Application
√ Licensed to Read Application
√ Licensed to Read Poster

11 READING AND SUCCEEDING: THE LIBRARY CARD CAMPAIGN AT THE LONG BEACH PUBLIC LIBRARY

The interest in, and the number of, library card campaigns in the later 1990s is not really surprising given changes in library technology often requiring new cards to be issued. Rather than issuing cards routinely, many libraries seized the opportunity to increase their visibility in the community. Such is the example of the Long Beach (California) Public Library. Due to change in computer systems in 1998, all Long Beach library users needed new library cards under the new system. At the same time, the library recognized that the changing nature of the community reflected a need to promote the library. Thus, the demographic changes in Long Beach linked with the library's new technology created an excellent opportunity for the library to develop a library card campaign.

During the 1990s, the City of Long Beach completed a community scan and undertook various studies in response to the perceived changing needs of the community. City departments shared information gathered from agencies such as the United Way, the *Long Beach Press-Telegram*, and the Long Beach Unified School District. The city's Health and Human Resources Department completed a community assessment that identified a growing ethnic population. Furthermore, 24 percent of the residents were born outside the United States and spoke a language other than English in their homes. The school district reported that more than 40 percent of the children in elementary school were classed as limited English proficiency students. In addition to reporting the growing number of languages, these agencies also reported increases in families under economic stress. More than 64 percent of the elementary school children were eligible for free lunches in the school district, and nearly 30 percent of the district students were from families on public assistance. The city was also experiencing a tremendous population explosion, causing a record school enrollment growth. The community assessment projected that between 1997 and 2000 population would increase by almost 10 percent. Clearly, the library administration decided, the demographic shifts mandated new, large-scale community outreach by all city organizations.

At the same time, national research began to highlight the literacy needs of youth. Locally, the *Los Angeles Times* newspaper inaugurated its "Reading by 9" program in summer 1998, and published article after article focusing on the need for strategies promoting student reading success rather than continued reliance on remediation programs. The Long Beach Unified School District instituted the third-grade reading initiative in June 1997, mandating that all third graders not reading at grade level participate in an intensive reading program in the summer months. The U.S. Department of Education and the National Center for Education Statistics provided reports on reading achievement indicating that children who are early and skilled readers have library cards, use the library regularly, and have books accessible in the home. Thus, the table was set, with an increasing interest in student achievement, to promote a new library card to teachers, students, and parents. The campaign would focus on the new electronic resources at the library as well as the more than 1.2 million books. With this track, the library could reposition itself as a partner in increasing student learning.

With the demographic changes in Long Beach and the reading research activities providing a dramatic backdrop, the Long Beach Public Library charted a new course in an era of intense and rapid technological change. The library crafted a public relations and marketing plan in 1998 to communicate to all residents the new state-of-the-art automated computer system, new electronic resources made possible by the new system, improved access to the Internet, and extensive print resources. The library card campaign emerged out of the marketing plan not just as one idea to promote the library, but rather as the top priority of the library's plan to increase its awareness in the community.

From this set of circumstances, the library developed the "Kids Who Read Succeed" library card campaign, targeting the over 75,000 students in grades K–12 in the Long Beach Unified School District. The goal of the campaign was to encourage youth literacy and promote use of the public library by placing a new library card and packet of library information into the hands of every student in the school district. The planning began not just by involving library staff; instead, the library's public relations and marketing committee invited several individuals representing outside organizations to participate in the planning process. The City of Long Beach's public information officer and the Long Beach Unified School District's director of public and employee information met with library staff representatives from the 12 Long Beach libraries over the course of several months to develop the library card campaign for implementation in the fall of 1998. The committee designed an approach to maximize the potential for student response by ensuring that library materials would be placed into every student's hands by a teacher.

The library set lofty, yet attainable goals from the beginning of the process:

- Double the established 3–6 percent response rate experienced in other library system card campaigns.
- Register 7,500 new Long Beach youth cardholders by the conclusion of the campaign.
- Reregister 7,500 current youth library cardholders.

One method to achieve these goals was to pay particular attention to areas where a large number of kids might not already have library cards. By focusing on several neighborhood libraries that served communities of new residents and large immigrant populations, the library was not only increasing the chances of successfully meeting the goals, but also extending services to populations most unaware of the services offered by free public libraries.

With that audience in mind, the city's public information officer penned a catchy slogan to publicize the newly designed, credit card–like library card: "Introducing Your New Long Beach Public Library Card. No Monthly Fee. Plenty of Interest." Rather than rolling out every element of the library card campaign at once as had been done in many systems, the card committee adopted a "teaser" format for the publicity. Under this plan, the library card and the slogan appeared in incremental stages in the different venues: on movie theater slides, on an electronic message board alongside the large interstate freeway, and on the library's delivery vehicle. The delivery van became, in effect, a moving billboard. The city offered to publicize the campaign in its publication *The Wave* which is available in three languages and is received by every household in Long Beach. The Long Beach Unified School District, the *Long Beach Press-Telegram* (a local newspaper), and the *Grunion Gazette* (a neighborhood-based smaller newspaper) were contacted to promote the forthcoming outreach. Much like the logo "hype" used years back for the movie

Batman, this approach was designed, as the slogan said, to build "plenty of interest."

The library's graphic artist began designing a special set of library information materials, and the public relations and marketing committee members established a budget to support the materials production and the publicity components of the campaign. The Friends of the Long Beach Public Library and the Long Beach Public Library Foundation approached local organizations with funding requests, and the Miller Foundation generously provided funding for all identified components of the campaign. The Employees Community Fund of Boeing, Office Depot, the Kiwanis Club of Long Beach, and the Friends of the Library contributed additional funding to pay for promotional materials and other related costs.

The campaign and its components were unveiled at the Long Beach United School District's September 1998 Back to School Rally, with the entire 5,000 district staff members in attendance. Launching the campaign at the rally was Long Beach Mayor Beverly O'Neill and Carl Cohn, superintendent of the Long Beach Unified School District. Mayor O'Neill presented the library card as "A Gift for Your Students," and the image of the new card was projected on large video screens behind the stages. The announcement was met with rousing applause, a great source of momentum and an energizing kickoff for the campaign.

The 75,000 library cards and information materials were assembled into packets. A unique student library card application form with a fold-over top complemented and highlighted the new library card. The library's map of library and school locations in the city was updated and redesigned to reflect the look of the library card. Bookmarks, packet labels, and new editions of the library hours flyer, were created using the design elements of the application and the slogans of the public relations campaign. Everything emerging from the library would carry the "Kids Who Read Succeed" message. Another key document in the campaign was a letter to parents from the mayor and the superintendent. They enthusiastically encouraged participation in the campaign and underscored the importance of reading for student achievement. The letter featured the logos of the city, the school district, and the library.

A campaign of this magnitude required more than just library staff. The volunteer coordinator of the Long Beach Public Library and the founder/coordinator of Long Beach Public Library's Junior Friends of the Library spearheaded a volunteer recruitment among the Long Beach high school youth to prepare the library information packets. Every weekend during September and October nearly 250 youth volunteers donated over 2,000 hours to compile the information packets. The volunteer workforce represented all ethnicities, all backgrounds, and all parts of the city. The visual impact of the industrious students at work, lined up at the many workstations in the Main Library lobby, weekend after weekend, was tremendous. By involving teens in the process, the library was continuing to generate interest among students before they actually received their applications—and to generate interest among high school students is an accomplishment, since they are one of the toughest audiences for any library card campaign to reach.

The school district's public information officer provided the library with information on the school's system for distributing materials, including classroom size standards for elementary, middle school, and high schools. Beginning in October 1998, the library delivery van transferred classroom sets designated for individual schools to the school district warehouse on a weekly basis. The district's delivery of each shipment proceeded the following week, beginning with the lower grades and progressing through the upper grades.

The response to the packets' arrival in local schools was immediate as youth library card applicants streamed through the libraries' doors. Some individual branch libraries needed augmented clerical hours to handle the increase in business. But the library soon learned there was more to come after hearing from numerous schools that the number of applications supplied was inadequate. The library learned that student enrollment figures had grown by 15,000 in the early weeks of school, and additional packet supplies were required. The rapid student enrollment in the fall of 1998 posed the greatest challenge to the campaign. The district struggled to cope simultaneously with an exploding student population and with student participation in the campaign. The library struggled with the supply of materials for an enlarged target audience and it struggled with the campaign packet delivery timeline.

Like many library card programs, the response and participation of teachers proved to be critical to the program's success. One elementary school faculty member passionately and successfully clamored for a district-supplied Spanish translation of the letter to the parents. Teachers chose to distribute materials at the best possible time for their students, to afford the materials the attention they merited. A front-page article in the *Long Beach Press Telegram* led to requests for library card campaigns in private schools and at the Long Beach School for Adults. The teacher response, the student response, the work of the Junior Friends of the Library, and the community support of the campaign ultimately led to extension of the campaign.

The Kids Who Read Succeed library card campaign far exceeded its goals, with a total response rate of 20 percent. New youth library customers who registered during the campaign (10,338) represented nearly a 100 percent increase over the previous year. In parts of the city where the community residents are *new* to the city, to the state, or even to the country, and where English is a second language to many, the increase was even more striking, with some libraries registering monthly increases of more than 400 percent. In addition, the campaign produced a 500 percent increase in reregistered youth. At the conclusion of the campaign, more than 66,500 Long Beach youth held new active library cards, and nearly 20,000 of these students were added in the four primary months of the campaign. Just as important, 68 percent of these new patrons have returned to the library to use the cards. An even more amazing fact is that 43 students have used their cards to check out 200 or more books, and one student has checked out more than 900 books since activating his new card.

According to the library administration, several effective components contributed to the spectacular campaign results. First, the partnership of the Long Beach Public Library, the City of Long Beach, and the Long Beach Unified School District created a powerhouse for youth, with marketing expertise combined with the long-standing effective relationship between the library and the school district. Second, the use of high school volunteers in the preparation of the packets of information promoted the visibility of the project in an audience of teenagers typically difficult to reach. The multiethnic volunteer corps also promoted the campaign in the minority communities less familiar with the library. Third, teacher distribution of the campaign packets proved extremely effective. Teachers demonstrated genuine enthusiasm for the outreach, facilitating student and parent participation at every juncture, from hosting library card parties at the local libraries to presenting the campaign packets on parents' days.

As happens in many library card campaigns, thousands of new library cardholders benefit, but also such campaigns increase the visibility of the library in the community. For example, as a kickoff to National Library Week, the Junior Friends of the Library were invited to appear before the city council, while the library director reported preliminary results of the campaign. The work of the Junior Friends contributed to the selection of Aaron Day, founder and advisor of the Junior Friends, as the City of Long Beach's Volunteer of the Year. Finally, the library has proudly received several awards for the campaign, including the Beach Cities Reading Association Literacy Award; the PRo Award, 2nd Place (Public Communicators of Los Angeles); the California Reading Association Literacy Award; the Savvy Silver Award (3CMA=City/ County Communications and Marketing Association); and the California Library Association PRexcellence Award. During deliberation of the proposed city budget, the council members and individuals in the community continually praised the work of the library, leading the mayor to exclaim that this was the "year of the library."

12 GETTING CONNECTED TO THE WORLD: THE LIBRARY CARD CAMPAIGN AT THE DURHAM COUNTY PUBLIC LIBRARY

The huge increase in technology has been a drawing card to bring many new users (particularly youth) into public libraries. Libraries have always connected people with information through books, but technology provides so many more opportunities for people to connect with the resources they need for recreation, education, or information. Knowing the strong appeal of technology, the Durham County Public Library, located in the "research triangle" in North Carolina, used increased technology access as the selling point to increase library card registrations during the fall of 1999.

The planning process began with a staff committee brainstorming ideas for a library card project. The committee consisted of staff from the branch libraries, the Main Library, and the bookmobile. The first "leap" was to realize that such a program needed to be anchored outside of the library. That meant finding community partners who could grant the library access to children, the main focus of the campaign. In particular, the library wanted to reach out to individuals and families who might not apply for a library card or might not even know what services the library offered. The staff was concerned that children in low-income families might most need the resources of the library. Thus, the library card campaign was also a project to work at bridging the digital divide. Further, the library was interested in reaching out to a growing Latino/Hispanic population. The staff came up with 25 possible community agencies that because of their location and heavy use, provided the best opportunity to reach these target markets.

One of the first partnerships was formed with the school system by piggybacking on an already successful school program.

The Durham Public Schools, like many school systems across the country, had targeted first graders for needing special help with reading. The Read First program provided community volunteers to visit first-grade classrooms to read to children. This was a program that the library already supported and in which several staff members were already volunteering. Working with this program, the library was able to offer every first grader a "Get Connected" plastic bag. The white bag featured a graphic of a blue globe connected to a plug with the slogan "Get connected to the world with your Durham County Library Card." Inside the bag, each child received a copy of a book, library card registration forms, a calendar of children's programs offered at the libraries, and a library card sign-up bookmark.

While this partnership reached out, it only targeted one grade. Many of the community agencies identified in the brainstorming session agreed to host an "open house" at their location, often in conjunction with another event, for the library to set up a table for registration. At each registration event, the site location would promote the visit in its newsletters and by other means. There was also media coverage of the outreach effort and a bookmark which listed all the locations. In addition, a new bookmark was produced with the graphic and slogan, listing the names, locations, and open hours of each library in the system. While not all of the community agencies were able to accommodate the library, several of those that did (such as a community health center, a Hispanic community center, and Boys and Girls clubs) provided the library with access to the children and families they were most interested in reaching.

In addition to working with community agencies, the library set up registration tables at community events (such as the Blues Festival, the Durham Alive concert, and Center Fest) and at the Carolina Theater. Even Barnes and Noble hosted a library card sign-up event, which included a visit by the library's mascot, Booker. At each registration site, anyone who signed up for a library card received the "Get Connected" bag. This bag contained a coupon for a free book at the library's upcoming book sale and coupons donated from various community partners (such as a Chick Fil-A coupon for free french fries). Other sponsors, such as bookstores and pizza places, added value to the library card by offering 10 percent discounts on merchandise and special meals during the month of September for all library cardholders. One of the most popular incentives was a two-for-one deal at a family fun park offered during National Library Card Sign-Up Month.

The biggest incentives, however, was that everyone who registered for a new card was entered into a drawing to win a computer. The computer, and other technology-related raffle prizes (such as CD-players and cameras), were donated by Ericsson, a large telecommunications company. The drawings for the prizes were held at the Technology Open House in October, which the Friends of the Library cosponsored with Ericsson. Any person who registered for a new card received an invitation to attend the open house.

Linking the new card with the open house provided the library with a showcase for many new technology products. A special "Get Connected to the World" handout was developed which listed the technology-based services and products found in the library, beginning with the early-learning computer centers in the children's room up to the computers on the third floor demonstrating the library's new genealogy resources Web page. In addition to showing off the technology to new cardholders, the open house also provided the library with an opportunity to recognize its technology donors, all of which were listed on the handout.

Although the program was only one month long, over 1,300 individuals applied for a card. More important, 78 percent of those new cardholders used their cards during the year. Over 150 of those new cardholders attended the Technology Open House. Of this group, 98 percent have used their cards and almost 20 percent have used it over 100 times. Through the Get Connected library card program and the Technology Open House, the library was able to introduce the library and its new technology to its patrons. Furthermore, the overall campaign greatly increased the visibility of the library in the community.

See the "Gallery of Successful Library Card Campaign Programs" for these documents from the Durham County Public Library:

√ Technology Open House Invitation
√ Get Connected to the World Bookmark

13 THE BEST OF THE REST: LIBRARY CARD CAMPAIGNS FROM LARGE URBAN AND COUNTY SYSTEMS

CLAYTON COUNTY, GEORGIA

The Clayton County Public Library campaign is a two-pronged approach, hitting schools as well as other outreach opportunities. For example, library staff have taken applications and brochures about library services to church events, health fairs, PTA meetings, pre-K parent meetings, Head Start meetings, and other places where children and parents gather together. After these events, the staff takes completed applications back to the library and then mails customers the library cards. In addition, the library focuses directly on those schools in its service area that the staff feels has a high percentage of library nonusers. The youth services staff person from each library visits each class in that school, reads and story tells, and then promotes getting a library card. Each school has a contest among its classes to see which class can get the highest percentage of library cardholders. Library card applications are left with each teacher with instructions for them to send them home with their students. The teachers return all completed applications by a due date to the school media specialist who compiles the percentages. The winning class at each school has a program presented by the youth services staff person (or someone from the community who has agreed to do a free program) plus snacks donated by local fast-food restaurants. Each winning teacher gets a small donated gift and the school media specialist gets a little gift for his or her extra work. The public library picks up the applications, completes the cards, and returns the cards to the school to send home with the students.

COLUMBUS, OHIO

Although not a system-wide effort, one branch of the Columbus Public Library (the Gahanna Branch Library) conducts its own campaign in the fall. During the campaign, called "The Best School Supply Is a Library Card," librarians from the branch visit first-grade classrooms. These visits can be very brief or span the length of a typical story time (30 minutes)—depending on what the teacher requests. The presentation ends with an invitation to the first graders to come to the library to get a library card or present their card if they already have one. When the students show library staff their card, they are given a free gift. This is a bag of items that includes a pencil, first-grade writing paper, a ruler, and an eraser. Like the library card, these are all items that contribute to literacy. The school with the highest percentage of first graders with library cards receives a $50 gift certificate to a local bookstore, courtesy of the Friends of the Library. The response rate the last year of the program was over 50 percent.

CONTRA COSTA COUNTY, CALIFORNIA

The Contra Costa Public Library system's "Contra Costa Reads 2000!" demonstrated the power of partnership and smart political positioning. The goal was to reach, over an 18-month period, every second grader in the library's service area. Targeting second graders was a sound political move which piggybacked on California Governor Gray Davis's initiatives to reduce class size in grades 1–3. Library card sign-ups were a cornerstone of this program which also involved increased outreach and visits to libraries. The library received a $25,000 grant from Pacific Bell to purchase paperback books to give to children as incentives to use the library and get library cards. These books would be given away during class visits which included story times as well as promotion of the library. The highlight of the visits, however, was the distribution of library cards to the students.

The campaign began with a kickoff celebration which included representatives from the involved school districts, the county board of supervisors, and from Pacific Bell. To show it was indeed a countywide effort, press conferences were held in three branch libraries during the day. Beginning in April 1999 each of the 23 branch libraries worked closely with the administrators, librarians, and teachers at one elementary school in their service area to get every child a library card. Building on those successes, the youth librarians at the branch libraries expanded the program with the goal of reaching every second grader by December 2000.

Teachers of second grade were given packets with information about the campaign, as well as enough library card applications, in both English and Spanish, for each student. The applications were distributed, and then returned completed to the teacher. The teacher would, often working with the school librarian, return the completed applications to the library. The library would then process the applications. The cards would be distributed during the class visits.

DES MOINES, IOWA

While almost every library card campaign is about motivating people to get and then use a library card, few libraries have attempted to increase use by directly attacking the barriers to access. One barrier to access, particularly for preteens and teenagers, is transportation. Unlike preschool story times or programs for younger children, programs for older kids often don't have a "role" for parents to play. In addition, rather than wanting to attend programs with parents, these kids want to go alone or with friends. Yet, in almost any community, getting to the library can be difficult or expensive. The Des Moines Public Library decided to attack the problem head-on by turning their library card into a bus pass. While not a formal library card campaign, the program achieves the same goals: to interest people in getting and then using a library card, in part because value has been added.

Working with the local transportation authority and other providers of summer programming for youth, the Des Moines Public Library created the "Do the Ride Things and READ" program. During the summer, persons under the age of 18 can go into any Des Moines Public Library and purchase a sticker for their library card for $30. Once attached, the library card turns into a bus pass which allows youth unlimited rides on city buses during the months of June, July, and August. As the cost of a regular monthly bus pass is $30, the program offers families a $60 savings. In addition to the sticker, they also get a map of the libraries and a calendar of summer activities. The library also arranged to distribute over 1,000 of the library card bus passes to low-income youth. During the first year of the program in 1999, the

Des Moines Metro Transit Authority reported 5,000 riders because of the program. By the next summer, that number had almost tripled, with 14,000 children and teens riding the bus by using their library card. The bus discount is only one perk of the value-added card, as the library also formed partnership with the city parks department and a science museum to offer half-price admission. The library also noticed that child care centers were participating in the program. The success of the project was a real boost for the collaborative summer programmers in Des Moines and Polk County. In addition to the library card allowing young people to ride the bus to get to and from summer programs, it also served the function of providing transportation for teens to get to and from their summer jobs.

JEFFERSON COUNTY, COLORADO

The main objective of the library card campaign at the Jefferson County Public Library in Colorado was really to increase the visibility of the library in the community. The library created a business reply form that includes a library card application to make it easy to obtain a library card. The cards were distributed at 30 back-to-school nights, through school library media specialists, at community parades and festivals, as inserts in daily and weekly newspapers, at speeches to community groups, and at every other opportunity. Library staff got the word out by attending the parades, festivals, and other events and by wearing special T-shirts that had the library card design on the front. Posters were used at tables at community fairs and in the foyer of libraries. A local TV station produced a public service spot promoting library card sign-ups for children. At the opening of a new branch library, the library honored their 300,000th library cardholder, a five-year-old girl, and used the occasion to promote the sign-up campaign.

See the "Gallery of Successful Library Card Compaign Programs" for this document from the Jefferson County Public Library:

√ Sign Up Today Application

LUMPKIN COUNTY, GEORGIA

Beginning with an aggressive program of outreach, including visits to PTA meetings at all the schools in the county, as well as visits to day care centers, the goal of the Lumpkin County Public Library was to motivate youth to get cards and to use them. The drawing card was, in fact, a drawing. Every time a customer used his or her library card, that person was allowed to sign up for a drawing. Thus, those who didn't have a card would need to get one and use it to be eligible for the drawing. The prize of the drawings was baskets filled with books, which were displayed prominently on the circulation desk. The library was able to obtain from the community enough book donations to give away one adult and one youth basket per day for a week. In addition, the Friends of the Library group gave money for the baskets and ribbon and tissue paper to make the book baskets attractive. The response was overwhelming as the drawing box was full almost every day. When people learned you could only enter if you had a card, they registered for one immediately, which led to a large increase in library card registrations.

Another aspect of the campaign was a partnership with Torrington, the business that had the most employees in the county. The library set up shop in the grounds of the business one day, making sure to be there during shift-change to improve exposure to employees. The partnership developed when the plant manager came to the library to donate a book about Torrington on behalf of the company. During the visit, he struck up a conversation with the branch manager about his interest in increasing the literacy rate among his employees. The branch manager followed up their conversation with a telephone call and together they decided to hold a "sign-up day" at the plant. He assigned an employee liaison to work with the library and they put together two large gift baskets, including books, a Torrington T-shirt and mug, and gift certificates. The only expense for the library was for the basket (the decorative ribbon was paid for again by the Friends of the Library). The Torrington factory had an in-house televised announcement system which was used to increase awareness about the upcoming card sign-up day, and to emphasize the drawing that would be held.

As the first few employees stopped to sign up, the plant manager chatted with them and shook hands and gave them a pat on the back. When employees signed up for a new card, or showed the one they already had, they were allowed to enter the contest for the gift baskets. Regardless of whether they won or not, 70 employees, which represents half of the total employees of the plant, were able to walk away from the table with a new library card right then. Staff reported that, later that day, families came into the library to make use of the new card that a parent had signed up for at work. The key to the success of the plant sign-up was having the "person in charge," the plant manager, so enthusiastic and involved with the project.

When talking to employees, library staff learned that many of them did not realize that library cards were free, did not know of the services the library offered, or did not even know the library existed. By reaching out into the community and becoming involved, the library not only registered more people for cards, but also had the opportunity to get to talk one-on-one about the difference libraries can make in the lives of citizens.

NEW ORLEANS, LOUISIANA

Creating a new library card often goes hand-in-hand with a library card campaign. The New Orleans Public Library, however, took the idea one step further by creating not only a new library card just for youth, but also a series of perks and incentives for getting the new card. The "Kids Club" program is a far-reaching program of the library designed to maintain children's interest in the library, to promote library programs and materials, to improve information literacy, and to expand youth involvement in the library.

Planning for the Kids Club began in the fall of 1999. Although open to all youth, the focus was on children ages 4 to 12. The two main products of the Kids Club are a quarterly newsletter and the new Kids Club card. The new card replaces the child's regular library card and has a bright look, with a yellow sun logo on a dark blue background. The special card, and the club concept, the library believes, will convey to youths a sense of belonging and exclusivity. As an incentive to get kids to sign up for the club, as well as to get youth back into the library, the library board agreed to waive fines up to $10 on every youth library card for the initial two months of the club. The waiver is only for fines, not fees or lost books.

See the "Gallery of Successful Library Card Campaign Programs" for these documents from the New Orleans Public Library:

√ Kids Club Newsletter
√ Kids Club Application

PHOENIX, ARIZONA

In his 1998 state of the city address, Phoenix Mayor Skip Rimsza challenged the Phoenix Public Library to distribute 25,000 library card applications to the over 1,000 first-grade classrooms in the city's 174 schools. His wife Kim was appointed the honor of chairing the campaign, which became known as "Project GOAL: Grade One at the Library." Mrs. Rimsza noted, "The importance of reading and a child's success as a reader is the cornerstone of his or her educational achievement. I can think of no more lasting legacy for a child than to motivate their family to make reading a daily part of their life. And I can think of no greater gift than a library card."

First-grade teachers distributed to their students applications written in English and Spanish. Students were instructed to take the application home and have their parents fill it out. Applications were returned to schools and soon after that the children received their GOAL cards. The card, designed especially for the program, featured a colorful design as well as the program's mascot, a dragon named "Bookbreath." The card was returned to the student in a special brochure, complete with a list of all branch libraries and a map. The colorful brochure offered the child congratulations from the mayor, his wife, and the library, and a reminder from Bookbreath to "Take good care of your card. Read every day." The brochure was available in both English and Spanish.

Project GOAL featured several incentives for first graders to use their card. The library increased holdings of beginning reader materials and children's classics to ensure that these new library cardholders would find something to check out. In addition, the library offered three "First Grade Family Super Saturday" programs across the system. These special programs featured not just story times but also guest performers and entertainers. In addition, the first time a first grader visited the library and used their card, he or she received a lanyard cardholder. On the second visit, first graders earned a specially designed book bag featuring the slogan and the mascot; the third visit earned them a Project GOAL pencil. Teachers received back, along with their students' cards, a poster where they could list the name of each student who signed up for a card, and chart the child's three visits to the library. The library also created a homework assignment for teachers to use, which involved asking students to visit the library with their parent or care giver. In the library, the assignment called for the student to find five items, such as magazines for kids, a video, a beginning reader, and other items of interest to first graders.

Teachers were the key to success of the program. Each first-grade teacher received from the library a simple instruction sheet, a sample script for introducing first graders to the program, a series of questions and answers, a map of all the library locations, and a colorful poster featuring the mayor, his wife, the mascot Bookbreath, and lots of smiling children holding up their GOAL cards. Teachers also received library card application forms for every student and a form for teachers to return the completed applications to the library, as well as a preaddressed, postage-paid envelope for submitting the applications. Teachers, too, were given incentives to participate in the GOAL program. Every teacher who returned applications was entered in a drawing to win one of 25 $100 gift certificates to a bookstore.

Teachers were also invited to contact the library to arrange for field trips to the library so first graders could use their cards. Knowing, however, the difficulty due to the cost of arranging for a bus to make such a trip, the library partnered with Valley Metro, the local public transportation agency, to provide free bus fares for class visits to the library.

The coordinated effort between the school and the library, coupled with the narrow but intense focus on one grade level led to a spectacular success. Over 73 percent of first-grade teachers in Phoenix participated and over 14,000 first graders got library cards. By the spring of 2000, 167 schools had received plaques for achieving 100 percent classroom participation.

See the "Gallery of Successful Library Card Campaign Programs" for these documents from the Phoenix Public Library:

√ Congratulations Brochure
√ Project GOAL Poster
√ Project GOAL Classroom Poster

PIKES PEAK, COLORADO

The campaign at the Pikes Peak District Library began with the branding of the library card as the "KNOWcard." Like the cards in the campaigns in Austin, Houston, and other large cities, the KNOWcard represented more than a library card campaign. The KNOWcard was to reposition the library into the thick of the educational structure, and also to integrate all parts of the library system in working toward a common goal. Using powerful words like "inform," "empower," and "inspire" as part of the key message, the significance of the library's mission was very clear: to have everyone in the community know the power of reading. A large part of the message was reminding parents and the public of the connection between library use and reading test scores. The library also pushed the concept that both reading and the library play a role in building assets in youth, and, thus, they help create a more literate, more informed community.

After naming a library card campaign project manager, the library hired work-study students for the campaign. In addition, the library looked outside of its walls for volunteers to help with a wide variety of tasks. For example, community groups were approached about projects to put together packets. A partnership was formed with the local chapter of the American Association of University Women to provide volunteers to assist with school visits. Integrating the library's volunteer program was just the beginning. The KNOWcard became the umbrella program for all activities with schools. While library staff had visited schools often in the past, that effort would now complement the KNOWcard campaign.

The focus of the campaign was on working with schools to sign up all students for library cards. Following administrative contacts with the 12 local school districts, library staff began contacting principals and media specialists. The key to success was creating a "fast and easy" method for schools to develop the program at their school. The program often began with a visit by a library staff member to speak at a faculty meeting or with the school library media specialist. The school and the library would agree on a date for a KNOWcard visit and the library then provided the schools with parent notification letters. These letters were sent home to parents via classroom teachers a week or so before a visit by the KNOWcard team. The letter stressed the importance of each child having his or her own card and touted all the benefits the card would provide for a child, in particular access to databases for homework help. Schools were also asked to promote the KNOWcard visit in their newsletters to parents. The library provided teachers with library card applications, in Spanish and English, as well as bar-coded library cards for each student.

On the day of the visit, library staff would "invade" the school, visiting up to ten classes at a time, and complete the registration process. The new, or replacement, cards were then activated within three days. To help encourage use of the cards, teachers were provided with a form to complete and return to the library requesting additional services, such as tours, library instruction, booktalks, or reading lists.

The visits are headed up by the branch manager. The team consists of a combination of five to six substitute staff and five to six volunteers. Some of the most efficient visits find the team registering an entire class of 30 students in ten minutes. The organized, well-planned visits to individual schools, with teams going class-by-class again and again netted huge numbers of library card sign-ups. While the goal is always to get every student a card, large library systems, for a variety of reasons, still have difficulty achieving 100 percent, in particular in the upper grades. Most of the Pikes Peak school visits, however, resulted in at least two-thirds of students receiving a KNOWcard.

In addition to the class-by-class visits, the KNOWcard campaign involved going out into the community. The most successful outreach events were those held at four Wal-Mart stores during National Library Week, resulting in the issue of over 400 cards, the majority of which were new, not replacement, cards. The first full year of the KNOWcard campaign saw library card registrations increase by over 50 percent in the first year. The goal for the first year of the campaign was to issue 23,000 new library cards. Almost twice that goal was achieved, as 45,350 new cards were issued in addition to 23,869 replacement cards. This huge increase, however, represents only one-third of the public schools targeted for the first year of the program. The goal, by the fifth and final year of the program is to have visited each of the 152 public schools served by the Pikes Peak District Library, as well as the 41 private and parochial schools. In addition, plans are under way to reregister the kindergarten and new students once their schools have been visited.

The branding of the campaign began with a redesign of the library card, turning it into a plastic KNOWcard. Distinctive typefaces were used on promotional pieces which were done in one of three colors (green, red, or purple). Slogans such as "Say yes to the KNOWcard" and "KNOW what? You can have your very own library card" were developed to be used in press releases and on promotional pieces.

A campaign of this scope also required developing improved methods of internal communication and methods of reporting information. By developing standardized reporting performance measures and setting unambiguous goals, all library staff had a clear idea of the expectations of the campaign.

An outgrowth of the library card campaign was a partnership with the local arts community. The library joined with an umbrella arts group, the Kennedy Center Imagination Celebration, to offer the "Teen Tickets to the Arts—It Takes Five" program. When high school students registered for library cards, they were given a special sticker which gave them access to local dance, music, and theater productions for only $5. Students who already had cards needed only to fill out an application to get the discount.

See the "Gallery of Successful Library Card Campaign Programs" for these documents from the Pikes Peak District Library:

√ Just Say "Yes" to the KNOWcard Brochure
√ KNOW What Brochure
√ KNOW the Power Brochure
√ KNOWcard Teacher Letter
√ KNOWcard Tally Sheet
√ KNOWcard Registration Process for Schools Flyer
√ KNOWcard Letter to Parents
√ KNOWcard Fact Sheet
√ Inform, Empower, Inspire Flyer

PRINCE GEORGE'S COUNTY, MARYLAND

Operating on the assumption that the only way to find new library users is to be outside of the library, the Prince George's County Library system launched in 1988 the "Library on the Move" campaign as a response to the first National Library Card Sign-Up Month. The library director (and future executive director of ALA) William Gordan, and his staff designed the campaign. In addition to resulting in hundreds of new library cardholders, the campaign also won an award for the County Public Library Relations Association. The library took a refurbished van and packed it full of paperback books, then hit the road. Not a bookmobile with a regularly scheduled route, instead the "Library on the Move" van toured the county over a ten-week period. The van stopped at every place people gathered, such as parks, malls, neighborhood celebrations, and even parades. All told, the library made 40 stops and registered over 1,500 new library cardholders in just ten days.

RAPID CITY, SOUTH DAKOTA

The Rapid City Public Library has been doing multiactivity library card campaigns in September for several years. But a convergence of forces (a new mayor, a new library director, a new public relations position, and a new television station) created a situation where increasing the visibility of the library became a strong possibility. The library card campaign developed as a very tangible, measurable, and highly attractive project to increase awareness. In addition, a political change allowed residents to register for library cards with no extra fee. The word would need to reach these new potential cardholders, as well as those in the city who still lacked cards.

Just as important politically was the full support of Mayor Jim Shaw. Not only did he support the library through funding, but also through public appearances on behalf of the library. One such appearance involved him having his hair dyed green. He vowed if a certain number of new library cards were issued, he would dye his hair the same color as the library card. Another year he challenged the library to sign up 650 new cardholders, which the library topped by coming in just shy of 900. As a reward, the mayor, working with a few local businesses, arranged for the preparing, and then consuming, of a 160-foot-long banana split. The mayor was heavily involved visiting schools, as well as doing radio and TV interviews. A new television station had just begun operating and became a key partner in the campaign. The new station, like the library, was looking to get the word out; the partnership to promote the library card, and thus promote the station, proved to be mutually beneficial.

SPOKANE, WASHINGTON

The Spokane Public Library celebrated National Library Card Sign-Up Month in 2000 by distributing library cards to all area first-grade students during the week of September 25–29. The library formed a partnership with the Spokane School District 81 and private elementary schools. Rather than merely handing out applications, the library actually distributed non-activated library cards to the children. In addition, each first grader received a colorful packet to take home, filled with information about the library, a map of the branch libraries, and a letter from the library director telling parents why and how to activate the cards. The goals of the program were to get every first grader a library card, to make them aware of the resources the library had to offer, and to remind parents about the importance of a library card throughout each child's academic career and beyond. Members of the library administration joined the youth services librarians to distribute the cards to approximately 2,800 students in 50 area schools. In connection with the distribution of library cards to first graders, Mayor John Talbott proclaimed September as Library Card Sign-Up Month in Spokane at the September 11 city council meeting.

VIGO COUNTY, INDIANA

By focusing a campaign on a small target group, the Vigo County Library was able to achieve big success. A staff team charged with developing the campaign saw that the greatest need for cards was among the youngest part of the population, so the group decided to target all kindergarten-age children in the county and all those preschool students who attended some of the larger preschool/nursery school agencies. At the same time, the library introduced five new library card designs to the general public and also waived the $1 replacement fee for a lost or damaged card.

The campaign kicked off in 1997 with a news conference at the Main Library, with the mayor proclaiming September Library Card Sign-Up Month in Vigo County. The library rented a bear costume ("Beary Bear") to serve as the mascot for the campaign. Beary Bear was present at news conference and a few other library events held during the month of September. He also visited elementary schools, seeing either morning or afternoon sections of kindergarten classes. One of the new card designs has a teddy bear and says "My First Library Card" on the front. The Friends of the Library purchased a large quantity of paperback books which were given to those children who brought a parent to the library to activate the new card.

The library also featured its new cards and Beary Bear at the annual Family Learning Day. This event for families, held at the Main Library, partners the library with over 50 local community agencies that set up booths to provide information. At the festival, people filled out the application form at the booth on the library lawn and then could come into the building and get their new card. The public liked having the choice of card designs (designs feature the teddy bear, a dinosaur, flowers, a B-52 plane, a Sherlock Holmes silhouette, a unicorn, and a plain card). Few chose the plain card, which makes sense, as there was nothing plain about the campaign in Vigo County to get preschoolers and kindergartners their first library card.

14 JUST BECAUSE SOMETHING IS TINY: WINNING LIBRARY CARD CAMPAIGNS FROM SMALLER LIBRARIES

BATAVIA, NEW YORK

The Richmond Memorial Public Library in Batavia serves a community of about 18,000 with three elementary schools with about 500 children in each. There are also three parochial schools with around 100 children in each one. The library card campaign begins by contacting each school and inviting them to participate in a contest. The competition is to see which public school and which parochial school can have the largest percentage of new registrations. The winner in each category gets several new books to add to the school library's collection. These books are purchased by the Friends of the Library. A letter is then sent to each teacher in the school stressing the importance of library cards and explaining the contest. Also included is a supply of library card applications which are attached to a note to parents explaining the advantages for their children in getting a library card. Teachers send the applications home to be completed by parents and returned to the school.

After a few weeks, library staff begin to visit each school and each classroom. During these visits, the staff members distribute the new library cards to students. This visit technique (rather than mailing the cards) affords library staff the chance to meet every teacher and every student. It also creates an "event" out of the student getting a library card. Students who still have not turned in their forms are thus given one more chance to do so. While this approach does take a great deal of staff time, the benefits are also great. The campaign resulted in nearly 90 percent of all students grades K–5 becoming registered for library cards. The library also encourages all kindergarten teachers to make a trip to the library. During that time, the young people get a tour of the library, hear a story, and sign up for library cards.

From the success of the library card campaign grew a program that further motivates and rewards young people for getting a card. When children sign up for a library card, the library keeps their applications and file them under the month of their birth. When their birthday rolls around, the library sends them a letter wishing them a happy birthday and congratulating them on getting a library card during the past year. They are invited to come to the library and pick a favorite book. The library then places a bookplate in the front of that book, with the inscription noting the young person's name and the birthday being celebrated.

Adults are not ignored, as every time adults register for a new library card they enter a drawing and the winner gets a free library bag donated by the Friends of the Library.

See the "Gallery of Successful Library Card Campaign Programs" for this document from the Richmond Memorial Public Library:

√   Happy Birthday Flyer

BERLIN, CONNECTICUT

The campaign conducted by the Berlin-Peck Memorial Library represents the power of strong school and public library cooperation. The campaign begins by children bringing their public library cards to school. The school librarian or classroom teacher checks off each child with a library card. For those children without cards, application forms are sent home. The forms are returned to the school where the public librarian picks them up periodically. Every classroom that has 100 percent of the children with library cards receives a book for the classroom, paid for by the public library. Copies of the book are also given to the school library since the school media specialist is often the "point person" in the school.

The campaign has been very successful, with 90–95 percent of all school children getting or having their cards. Teachers became very enthusiastic about the campaign, even having library card application forms at parent/teacher conferences for parents to fill out. Classroom teachers love getting a book for their classroom. The first time the school and the public library worked together on the program was during the *Waldo* book craze, so getting more copies of the books into the schools was helpful. During the last campaign, teachers could choose from the *Magic School Bus* titles,

Magic Eye titles, and *I Spy* titles. The funding for the first campaign was from a local grant, the second campaign was funded through the library's programming budget.

Like many successful library card programs, this campaign has created new library card users and also strengthened the relationship between the school and the public library. One outgrowth of the program is that when children register for kindergarten, they receive, in the public school registration packet, a letter from the library inviting parents to get a library card for their child. The bottom half of the letter is a registration form. This program, in addition to inspiring many parents to bring their kindergartners into the library to get their first library card, also led to adults rediscovering the library and getting cards of their own. The cost for the library is very low—only the photocopying of the letter and some postage for mailing library cards.

CARROLLTON, OHIO

One key to successful library card campaigns is finding the right partners to provide access to youth. The Carrollton County Public Library found two such partners to help them put kids and cards together. The first is a program in the middle school, located across the street. Once a month, the library invites all the seventh-grade language arts classes to come to the library for a program, such as storytelling, poetry, or a scavenger hunt. Students are also given free time to find and check out materials. There is a big push each September to ensure that every seventh grader in the school system has a library card. Applications are given to the language arts teachers who distribute them to students to take home for signatures. The signed applications are returned to the teachers and then picked up by the library. Students get their cards before or at the first visit. A major reason for the program's success is working with students who have inactive or blocked cards. The library does everything possible to make sure that a card gets into the hands of every seventh grader. The first year of the program saw only one language arts teacher participate, but, over time, all have come on board, so that every student now gets a card and visits the library.

Another library card campaign involves the youngest patrons. The library developed newborn packets, which contain a library card application and a letter of congratulations to the parents of all newborns in the county. Parents are invited to bring the application in to get a card for their new baby and for themselves. To make the program work, the library had to change its policy regarding library cards, which had required a signature from the cardholder. The success of the program hinged on partnering with the county health department's visiting nurse program. The visiting nurses visit the homes of every newborn and they provide the library packet, in addition to other parenting information. The success of the program led to a grant received by the library to buy bags, bibs, and copies of *Read to Your Bunny*, by Rosemary Wells, to be part of the kit.

DICKSON, TENNESSEE

Library card campaigns are often conducted in September to tie in with back-to-school preparations of parents and children, but the Dickson County Library took a different approach by looking at the library card not as a school supply, but rather as a gift for parents to give their children. The library began a small campaign in December a number of years ago encouraging parents to give their children library cards for Christmas. The library even provided the stocking! The library director and her assistant spent a day making small, red felt stockings to distribute with each card issued as a gift. It was suggested that they be hung on the tree. The program was so well received that a local FCE group (Home Demonstration Clubs) took over the project and made the stockings. For several years, the library had children pull their card out of the little red stocking when they came to check out their books. Some of those stockings got very ratty looking before they gave out.

EVANSTON, ILLINOIS

The Evanston Public Library created a new library card campaign and added a strong library card component to existing grant-funded programs, such as a partnership with a school district to do outreach to the Hispanic community funded by the Illinois Secretary of State. In addition, the library received an LSTA grant for the "Books Alive!" program which specifically targeted areas of the cities where, based on library card registration and use, the community was not actively involved in the library. Finally, library card sign-up became an important component of the library's BabyLove program which featured deposit collections of library materials available for checkout at the health department and a well baby clinic. Part of the program was an activity card that encouraged and rewarded customers for using the library.

Just as innovative, however, was the library's use of parent-teacher associations (PTAs) in the library card drive. Library staff trained PTA volunteers to do library card registration. Then, during the kindergarten registration process at various city elementary schools, parents would have the opportunity to sign up their children for library cards as they were filling out other forms. In this way, parents were already in form-signing mode, with their IDs ready. The PTA volunteers then returned the applications, which were in both English and Spanish, to the library. The library staff then mailed the cards to the new customers, or, if an entire class had signed up, the cards were returned to the teacher to distribute. The PTA represents a group of concerned and dedicated parents who know the value of education, and thus the value of library cards. By involving them directly, not only did it save the staff time from visiting each school, but also it gave the PTAs a stake in the success of the program.

FOUNTAINDALE, ILLINOIS

The Fountaindale Public Library District conducts an extensive card sign-up during the month of September and October called "Battle of the Cards." The program is aimed at grades K–5 and conducted in both library buildings. The students come in with a form that is filled out with their library card number, name, and name of their school. The school with the highest percentage of returns based on their enrollment wins a paperback book collection valued at $200 and purchased by the Friends of the Library. Students that already have a card participate as well as those that get new cards. To coincide with the 30th anniversary of the library, the campaign was expanded to reach adults.

The Battle of the Cards is a cooperative program between the library and the Valley View School District. The campaign began with a letter sent to schools announcing the Battle of the Library Cards campaign. Another letter is composed, run off, and handed out to students to take home to their parents. Each school is contacted by the library to organize a promotional visit. Depending on the situation of the school, the library either visits individual classrooms or combined grades for a Battle of the Cards assembly. During the assembly, there is a prop of an oversize library card to show students what a card looks like. The library also explains during the assembly the letter and form that will be taken home, the length of time students have to return the entry form to their school, filling out the entry form, and the fact that a library card application is attached to the letter and can be used for applying for a first-time library card. Time is also given to answer questions about the campaign and the library.

The promotion doesn't end there, however, as teachers, administrators, and school librarians have been cooperative in trying to help get the message out. As most of the school libraries have such a small book budget, a $200 paperback book collection means a great deal and they try to encourage students to return the forms. In addition to the 12 public schools served by the library, the campaign is also taken into the 2 parochial schools served by the library. The library offers a small gift, such as a notepad, stencil rulers, or the like as an incentive to have students bring their forms directly to the library. The belief is that once students come in and see the library facility, they will want to return.

See the "Gallery of Successful Library Card Campaign Programs" for this document from the Fountaindale Public Library:

√   Battle of the Books Flyer

JACKSBORO, TENNESSEE

Rather than marrying their library card campaign to a library event, such as National Library Week or even National Library Card Sign-Up Month, the Jacksboro Public Library used the national Kids Day America celebrated each September. Kids Day America is a project dedicated to health, safety, and environmental education of the community's children. A combined community celebration and health fair, the event was held at a local shopping center and sponsored by a local chiropractor. The library set up a table, complete with a banner inviting children to get library cards. The library created, based on materials from the ALA Web site, bookmarks and flyers to hand out to children as they made their way around the tables to the fingerprinting station. Library signature cards were given as handouts along with the bookmarks and flyers. Some parents completed the applications right at the table, while others brought the application into the library after the event. In addition to library staff working the booth, the president of the Friends of the Library also assisted in the distributing of materials and library card registration forms.

JESSAMINE COUNTY, KENTUCKY

In addition to having a focused library card campaign, the Jessamine County Library attempts to make every library card sign-up for a child an event. For each child who gets a new library card, a staff member uses the library's digital camera to take a picture of the child with the first book he or she checked out. The photos are then printed, laminated, and displayed on a window near the children's library. This program has generated a lot of interest among the kids and their families.

The more formal campaign was a competition during September among all the elementary schools in the district to see which school had the highest percentage of students with public library cards. As a part of the campaign, the library had a prize drawing at the end of the month. All elementary-age library cardholders could enter, but they had to come to the library to do so. The prize was a concert by a children's musical group held in the winning child's classroom. This competition went over really well and generated a lot of interest.

MISSOULA, MONTANA

The Missoula Public Library conducted a major library card campaign in September 2000 that represents a community-wide effort involving local government, schools, and the business community. A variety of activities and events were created to generate interest and increase library card registration. As part of the campaign kickoff, the mayor issued a proclamation for the library declaring September Library Card Sign-Up Month. The library solicited local merchants and groups to donate items for weekly prize drawings. New cardholders had the chance to put their name in for the drawing and win one of the prizes. Several local merchants increased their commitment by offering discounts ranging from 5 percent to 20 percent when library cards were presented, for both new and existing cardholders.

Within the library, interest was generated through a series of contests. One of the most popular was "guess how many library cards in a jar"; the winner, who needed to have a library card, scored a huge Paddington bear. The library also sponsored a writing contest, "Why I Love My Library Card." Winning entries were published in the library's newsletter as well as the local newspaper. Grand prize was a $100 gift certificate to the mall.

In an effort to get back old users with blocked cards, the library sponsored a "Food for Fido" campaign cosponsored with the Humane Society. The idea was to encourage those with fines to pay off their fines with a donation of pet food or toys and start using the library again. As another incentive, the library also gave away magnets shaped like a book with the library's logo and contact information. This was for patrons to stick on their refrigerators to hold the printout of materials and due dates.

The card campaign began with a small staff committee brainstorming ideas on how to increase the number of registered borrowers. For a variety of reasons, a formal partnership with schools did not occur although several school librarians did support and promote the sign-up campaign. The library also sought out other locations where parents and children might gather, focusing on public buildings such as health clinics.

See the "Gallery of Successful Library Card Campaign Programs" for these documents from the Missoula Public Library:

√ Proclamation
√ Food for Fido Flyer
√ Winning Contest Entries

MOORESVILLE, INDIANA

One reason that library card campaigns take place in September is to remind the public that for school-age children, a library card is an essential supply for their school success. With the help of a local sponsor, the Mooresville Public Library used this idea as the hook of its campaign, offering a back-to-school supply kit with every new student card. This small, yet powerful incentive, got the attention of a lot of parents who brought in their children to sign up for cards. During a previous campaign, the library gave away an art supply packet with every new student card. In addition to promoting the campaign to parents, the library also works with schools by sponsoring a pizza party to every classroom in the school district that is able to get 100 percent of students signed up for a library card.

NEWPORT BEACH, CALIFORNIA

Rather than launching a year-long or even month-long campaign, some libraries, like the Newport Beach Public Library, focus their energy and efforts on one big event to generate maximum publicity and participation. The library formed a partnership with Fashion Island, a local shopping mall, for a one-day celebration in conjunction with the national Read Across America Day commemoration of Dr Seuss's birthday on March 2. The event, called "A Library Card for Every Kid," was held on Saturday, March 3. Fashion Island is an outdoor mall and one of the courtyards was set aside for the library to set up tables to register children and their families for library cards. But in addition to offering card registration, the event showed the library in action with several story times throughout the afternoon. The festival atmosphere was completed with a face-painting station, the distribution of balloons to children, and a visit by costumed storybook characters (provided through a partnership with the local Barnes and Noble). In addition to signing up fellow youth at the registration tables, youth volunteers from the Library Young Adult Advisory Council filled the character costumes, handed out balloons, and did the face painting. Merchants within the mall also partnered with the library by donating goodies and giveaways to hand out as part of the event.

NILES, ILLINOIS

A close relationship with the local chamber of commerce provided the Niles Public Library with the starting point for their library card campaign. The library learned that a new pizza chain had recently joined the chamber and opened an outlet in Niles.

Assuming, correctly, that the new business would be looking for ways to promote itself, the library approached the manager about a partnership to increase the visibility of the library and of the pizza parlor. The two teamed to launch a library card campaign. Each teen or adult who registered for a library card during the month of September received a coupon for a free personal pizza at this restaurant. Teen or adult customers who already had a library card could show the card at the restaurant in September and receive a free dessert. For younger children the library offered such giveaways as puzzles and bubble pens as incentives. The campaign was promoted by the pizzeria, the library, and the chamber of commerce. The response was fantastic, with over 250 new patrons registered in just one month.

OSHKOSH, WISCONSIN

What happens when you combine a library with a long history of outreach and collaboration, a library director with the mind of a futurist, and a new school superintendent looking to make a mark? In Oshkosh, this recipe cooked up a wildly successful library card campaign. As the library was engaging in strategic planning, a clear initiative emerged to become a leader in the community in supporting reading among youth. Following the presentation about the Power Card at the Public Library Association conference in March 2000, Laurie Magee, the head of children and family outreach services for the library realized that a library card campaign would be a powerful project to demonstrate the library's reading initiative in action.

Given an existing library card posting the images of two lions, the campaign transformed into the "Wild Card" campaign, which urged young people to take a library card with them so as not to get lost in the information jungle. The superintendent of the Oshkosh Schools was not only new, but also a member of the library board, thereby creating a perfect opportunity for the schools to support the project. Working with the schools, the library staff visited every elementary school to present a skit and distribute library card applications. The applications contained the Wild Card graphics as well as a note to parents. Each parent was asked to check if their child had a card, had a lost card, or needed a card for the first time. Elementary teachers collected the completed applications from students and returned the applications to the library, which, in turn, returned them to the students, sometimes by revisiting schools. The big incentive for schools to participate was the offer of free milk and cookies for every class that achieved a 100 percent sign-up. A local grocery store chain, Copps, that the library had worked with on other projects, donated the milk and cookies. Four schools—three public and one parochial—got 100 percent participation for every class, earning not only the treats, but also a performance by a local folk singer at the school, paid for by the library. By the end of the program in October 2000, the number of elementary school students with cards increased from 69 percent to over 90 percent in just two months.

For secondary schools, the program was slightly different. Visits were not made and students were encouraged to return the applications themselves. The incentive for many of these students was financial: if they got a new card during the months of the project, the replacement card fee would be waived. As well, any fines would also be forgiven, although students would still be accountable for lost or missing items. While this promotion was open to all youth, students in the secondary schools took full advantage and, in doing so, many started using the library again. Finally, the library also worked with the schools as children were being screened for kindergarten to ensure that children started school with a library card in hand.

The Wild Card campaign accomplished several objectives. Not only did it get lots of kids library cards, it also strengthened the partnership between the schools and the library. Moreover, it also demonstrated that, unlike many of the library's strategic plans, this one had legs—for the vision to be reached, the library would undertake programs aimed to turn words into actions. But just as important, as in many other library card campaigns, was the effect of the program on library staff. During one of the visits to schools, a veteran staff member of the circulation department received from one elementary schooler a large hug and an even larger smile. The staff member noted that doing the program—going out into schools and putting library cards in the hands of children—served as a nice reminder of how important getting a library card was in the life of a child. In bringing value to the life of a child, a staff member (like any involved in a library card campaign) adds value to the community, and to his or her own life as well.

OTTAWA, OHIO

Unlike many library card campaigns focusing on getting kids ready for school with library cards, the campaign of the Putnam County Public Library focuses on getting kids ready for summer reading. The goal is to ensure that each first grader has his or her own library card before the library's summer reading program begins in June. The campaign is done through the schools and starts in the fall. The library begins by sending letters to the principals officially inviting their first graders to visit the library. While many teachers have been making these visits for years, working through the principal ensures support for these visits from the very top of the school. The library has almost total participation with first graders visiting the main library and the seven small branches. Students are provided with a tour of the building and a story time, and then each child is given the opportunity to choose one book to check out and take home. Prior to the visit, the library sends home letters to the parents and registration cards. The school acts as a "verifier" for the parent address and other information on the application. During the visit, the cards are distributed, which turns into a real celebration. Very seldom does a parent not comply; usually the only first graders who do not get a card the day of the visit are those who already have one. While results may vary from year to year and from principal to principal, for the most part this program ensures that all first graders in Putnam County get a library card and therefore are ready to participate in the summer reading program.

See the "Gallery of Successful Library Card Campaign Programs" for this document from the Putnam County Public Library:

√   Dear Parent Letter

PEMBERVILLE, OHIO

The need for library card campaigns is spurred on by a variety of factors, but all revolve around increasing access to collections. Two of the keys to increasing that access for youth are improving cooperation with schools and enhancing youth's ability to identify, locate, and then obtain materials. The Pemberville Public Library's card campaign emerged from an LSTA grant which allowed the library to purchase computers for each of the school libraries in the Eastwood school system. The purpose of these computers was to give the schools access to the library's online catalog. Catalog access, however, was not the only thing students needed. The library next developed a routing system between the library and the schools. This system enabled students to request and check out public library books while at their schools. For this innovative program to succeed, students would need library cards, but upon investigation, the library discovered that quite a few students did not have library cards. Working with the schools, who were eager to see the cooperative venture succeed, the library sent library card applications to each class. The teacher distributed the applications and then collected completed applications from students. The applications were then forwarded to the library to provide cards to all the kids who didn't have them previously. The library cards were sent back to the schools to be distributed by classroom teachers. Overall, over 700 new library cards were issued in a fairly small school system with four elementary schools, one middle school, and one high school. Once all students had cards, then the vision of the LSTA grant could begin to be realized.

PERRY COUNTY, OHIO

Small things make a difference. A huge part of any library card campaign is not only signing people up for cards, but also removing the obstacles that may have prevented users from getting cards in the past. Such was the case at the Perry County District Library where the campaign was simply making a policy change in order to increase children's/young adults access to library cards. The library board changed the policy which had required that a parent/guardian come in to a library to complete and sign an application for his or her child. With the policy changed, the library was able to visit many faculty meetings at the local schools. At these meetings, the library distributed library card applications with letters of welcome for the teachers to distribute to their students. By issuing cards via teachers and schools, the library dramatically increased access for youth in the county by issuing an estimated 2,000 cards, a huge number for a rural county.

RANCHO CUCAMONGA, CALIFORNIA

The library card campaign at the Rancho Cucamonga Public Library was a precursor to a new program of offering bookmobile services to schools. The campaign got students registered for library cards so they could use the bookmobile, and, just as important, it got them excited about using the library. Thus, when the bookmobile made its first visit, youth could spend time finding materials rather than filling out forms. The campaign began with a letter to over 20 school principals with invitations to call the library to learn how their school could participate. Those schools that did not respond were contacted by the library.

The key to the success of the program was flexibility. Rather than having one set way of doing the campaign, the library adapted the drive to meet each school's preference. The library staff attended student assemblies, teacher meetings, school library staff meetings, and individual classrooms during the school day. In the evening, staff would attend open houses for students and their parents. Most important, the library staff pitched the program at a district-wide meeting. Information about the campaign was also widely distributed via a back-to-school article in a city-published quarterly magazine.

While the schools differed somewhat in how they promoted the drive, in most cases the campaign began with the library providing hundreds of applications for each school. The applications contained a short letter to parents stressing the importance of reading and of having a library card, and how both can affect a child's success in school. Teachers distributed the letters and applications in class. Students returned them to school at a central location chosen by the school. The library provided each school with the ALA-sponsored poster featuring Marc Brown's Arthur to mark the collection point. School staff would contact the library when a number of applications had been returned and the library staff would visit the schools to pick up the applications. In some cases the schools merely mailed the applications to the library.

The applications were brought back to the library where the circulation staff entered the data and completed the process. The cards were then mailed to the parents of the applicant along with a letter introducing the library. Included in the letter was a small premium for the child, such as a sticker or food coupon, donated through partnerships with local merchants. If, during the process, the staff discovered that the applicant already had a card, a different letter was sent which explained what to do if a card had been lost.

The library administration and the board of trustees are very pleased with the results, which saw library card registrations increase 38 percent over the previous year. Library staff believes that the support of the school principals helped make the program such a success. Through the information provided to the principals, the library was able to remind these educators of what a valuable resource a library card would be for their students.

RANDOLPH COUNTY, GEORGIA

The Randolph County Library serves a population of 8,000 and there is only one elementary school. The campaign was conducted in September as a contest between classes in the school to see which class would be the first to get 100 percent sign-ups. The prize for the first class to reach 100 percent was to receive a pizza party. To promote the program, the librarian cut out large, round poster-board circles to look like pizzas, and then small orange circles to resemble pepperoni. Every student who got a library card had his or name written on a pepperoni. Each week during September, the librarian would take the pepperoni to the school office. They were sorted by teacher's name and put into Ziploc bags. Each week during the school announcements the school principal would tell which class was in the lead. It created a lot of excitement in the school and the campaign added 335 new library customers.

RIMERSBURG, PENNSYLVANIA

The Arthur theme set by ALA for National Library Card Sign-Up Month in September 2000 inspired many libraries to start campaigns; Arthur is an attraction for younger children. At the Eccles-Lesher Memorial Library, the campaign had two goals: to supply as many people with library cards as possible and to have them use their cards. The centerpiece of the plan was to design and promote activities for the kids using the Arthur brand, including a large Arthur celebration. In addition to promoting the campaign in the local newspaper, the library also utilized its own publication, a kids' newsletter. This publication is unique because the editor is a senior at the high school and the ten reporters are also all youth (two from the high school, five from fourth through sixth grades, two from the third grade, and one home schooler). The library also printed up invitations and handed them to kids when they were checking out books. Ads were also placed on the local access TV channel and flyers were distributed in the library and the local businesses.

For the event, the library staff created a poster-board library card that resembled the library's real cards. Since Arthur was the mascot for this campaign, the library staff also made a large Arthur from poster board to hold the card; Arthur and the card were then placed in the library's front window. These items were on display for the whole month of September, encouraging everyone who did not have a library card to come in and get one. Inside the library, there was a display of Arthur books. The event itself was an Arthur celebration, including a birthday party for Arthur. The children's librarian read Arthur books to the kids, and did crafts making party hats and birthday cards for Arthur. An Arthur sticker book was used as a door prize. There was also a "How well do you know Arthur and his friends?" quiz, where kids received a fancy pencil for each right answer. Everyone sang "Happy Birthday" to Arthur and had cupcakes and a drink. On the way out, as a thank-you gift for attending and getting a library card, children were given Arthur book bags, bookmarks, coloring pages, and a list of Arthur books.

SCOTTSBLUFF, NEBRASKA

The Scottsbluff Public Library is a small library that developed an aggressive campaign called "Kindercarding," which occurs annually during National Children's Book Week in November. The library cosponsors the project with the local newspaper and targets every local kindergartner. Library staff visits every kindergarten class to explain, promote, and give children their "Kindercard" initiation.

SPRINGFIELD, ILLINOIS

One method not only to increase the number of library card-holders, but also to encourage customers to renew their cards and to increase library traffic is to add value to the traditional library card. The Lincoln Library in Springfield, Illinois, developed a value-added approach with their "Show Us Your Library Card Campaign." During September 2000 library cards served "double duty," allowing customers to use them to check out materials as well as to receive gifts and discounts from participating merchants. The library signed up over 20 local retail establishments, including fast-food titans (such as Burger King and Subway) and locally owned pizza and taco shops. The library also worked with florists, an antique mall, and video stores. For the participating vendors, the program demonstrated their support for the library and gave them visibility among the 50,000 library cardholders. The program was based on a similar promotion the library held during its centennial celebration.

WASHINGTON-CENTERVILLE PUBLIC LIBRARY, OHIO

In September 2000, as part of National Library Card Sign-Up Month, the Washington-Centerville Public Library held an Arthur event. The library borrowed an Arthur costume from a local bookstore, and built the program around a library visit by the costumed character. As families arrived, the library staff distributed numbers, just like in a bakery, to ensure that everyone got a chance to see Arthur. Children were also given an Arthur coloring exercise while they waited their turn to visit. The event included an Arthur character visit, Arthur stories, Arthur and friends coloring pages and crafts, a guessing-jar contest, and free bookmarks. The publicity for the event encouraged parents to apply for library cards for their children and to bring along cameras to take snapshots. The library created 8-by-24-inch posters and 8½-by-11-inch signs to promote the event.

The library estimated that over 700 people attended the event. Circulation for the day was 144 percent above normal for the day, and applications for new cards were 42 percent above normal. The planning for the event centered on the Arthur character and not on any individual station at the event, so signing up for a card was certainly an important offering that day, but it was just one of several things to draw families to the library. Schools were involved as they are for all library events: they were notified in advance so that they could announce the event in their newsletters.

See the "Gallery of Successful Library Card Campaign Programs" for this document from the Washington-Centerville Public Library:

√   Program Flyer

15 A TICKET TO READ: THE STATEWIDE LIBRARY CARD CAMPAIGN IN SOUTH CAROLINA

While many state libraries have pushed library card campaigns, these have often been aimed at getting people to sign up for, or become aware of, statewide library cards. The professional literature is filled with information about statewide library cards, but an innovative and exciting program from South Carolina actually aims to increase public library card registration for children throughout the state. The campaign came at the urging of Governor Jim Hodges who, in his first state of the state address, said, "We need to teach our children that the most valuable possession a kid can have is not a new pair of Nikes or a Game Boy . . . it's a library card" (*Ticket to Read*, 2000:5). Literacy, reading, and libraries were also subjects of great interest to Rachel Hodges, the first lady of South Carolina. Thus the stage was set to develop a statewide library card drive in a state where less than 50 percent of children have their own library cards.

The South Carolina State Library, the South Carolina Association of School Librarians, and public libraries kicked off the statewide library card campaign called "Ticket to Read" at a ceremony in February 2001 at an elementary school in the capital city of Columbia. The Ticket to Read program is directly targeted to elementary school children, and ran until the beginning of National Library Week in April. The timing was excellent since, in a recent national news story of a brother and sister from Columbia who each scored a perfect 1600 on their SATs, their parents said that the secret to academic success is simple: take your children to the public library on a regular basis.

The state library partnered with Clemson University, McDonald's, South Carolina Association of Cable TV Operators, Step into Reading, and the University of South Carolina (USC) to spread the message across the state that every child should have a library card. The kick-off featured a preview of public service announcements produced by South Carolina Educational Television, starring University of South Carolina and NBA basketball great Alex English, South Carolina native Leeza Gibbons, and

African American poet Gienis Redmond. The cable TV operators and other commercial stations broadcast the public service announcements.

Clemson University and USC promoted the campaign throughout their athletic teams. As part of the Ticket to Read campaign, both schools designated two men's home baseball games as "Show Your Library Card and Get in Free" games. At the first USC game, the public address announcer told the audience:

> Fans, the South Carolina State Library would like to thank everyone who used their library card to get into tonight's game. If you don't have one, make sure to pick one up by April 11th when you'll be able to show your library card prior to the Citadel game and receive free admission. Reading can be one of the great joys in life and the South Carolina State Library would like you to know that a free library card—available at any public library—is your ticket to read.

In addition, the radio networks for both schools' athletic programs aired public service announcements (PSAs) during baseball games and coach call-in shows. One of the PSAs was done by USC sports announcer Charlie McAlexander.

McDonald's distributed specially designed tray liners in all participating restaurants. The tray liner featured the Ticket to Read logo, and told kids how they could get a free library card, stressing the term free. The tray liner also promoted summer reading and hyped the wide variety of services and resources available to elementary school-age children. McDonald's restaurants across the state provided free coupons for children who got a new library card. In addition, Ronald McDonald himself was the star of one PSA.

Ticket to Read was piloted in the spring of 2000 in six counties. As a result of the program, over 1,600 elementary students got library cards for the first time. For the statewide campaign, superintendents of each school district received a letter from James B. Johnson, Jr., the director of the South Carolina State Library, and Betsy Adams, the president of the South Carolina Association of School Librarians. The letter outlined the Ticket to Read program, focusing on the advantages to students. In particular, the letter promoted the DISCUS project, which is South Carolina's Virtual Library, and how a library card could provide access to a wide variety of databases found on this service.

The letter was followed up by a letter sent to each elementary school principal, with a copy of that letter going to each school library media specialist. The school librarians, however, got much more than a letter from the state library to help them with the Ticket to Read program. They got a handbook written by Penny Hayne, the media specialist at Lake Murray Elementary School in Lexington and the past-president of the South Carolina Association of School Librarians, and Jane Connor, the children's services consultant at the South Carolina State Library. The handbooks contained such items as:

- A sign-up poster
- Authors' and illustrators' birthdays taking place during the program
- Suggested story times with a library theme
- Winning poems from the "Why I Love My Library" contest (sponsored by ALA)
- Story-time selections for young and older children about libraries, books, and reading
- Enrichment activities for teachers and parents
- Handouts such as a doorknob hanger and library-related puzzles
- Camera-ready art

But perhaps the most important parts of the handbook were those providing instruction and ideas for making the Ticket to Read campaign work in every school.

The instructions described how each school media specialist might use the various materials. The sign-up poster, for example, went to every homeroom teacher. It provided space at the top to list the name of the county library the students would use and the name of the teacher. The poster had one column for students to sign their names at the start of the program if they already had a card. The second column (labeled "I just got a library card!") was for students who got a card as part of the Ticket to Read to sign their names. The goal of every classroom, of course, was to get every child's name on the poster by April 13. At the end of the campaign, media specialists collected the posters from the classrooms and filled out the reporting form documenting the number of children who got cards during the campaign. The school in each district with the highest percentage of children getting library cards during the campaign received a book signed by the first lady of South Carolina.

Another important part of the handbook provided to each school was a section of ideas for promoting the Ticket to Read program specifically, and for reading/library use generally. Ideas included the following:

- Use the "Suggested Story Times with a Library Theme," "Winners! Why I Love My Library Card Contest," and bibliographies for younger and older children in this handbook for ideas for media center activities. Pass the ideas on to classroom teachers.
- Send home copies of some or all of the camera-ready parent handouts during the campaign. (There were two versions of a "Helping Your Child Enjoy Reading" handout. One had more detail than the other. Librarians were urged to choose the one more suitable for the school population.)
- During the 1999–2000 school year, the PBS *Arthur* series, based on the books by Marc Brown, used a focus on libraries and the joys of reading. For some fun activities that encourage reading, go to the Arthur Web site: www.pbs.org/wgbh/Arthur.
- Provide posters in every classroom and use any extras in strategic places around the school, such as the media center, school entrance, or cafeteria.
- Do a bulletin board about the campaign. One simple idea is to draw a large library card and ask, "Did you know that a library card is a Ticket to Read? Get yours at the public library."
- Include information about the library card campaign in your school newsletter. Perhaps a parent or student who is a regular user of the local public library could write something for the school newsletter.
- Talk on in-school broadcasts about the library card campaign and how students benefit from having a library card. A brief comment by a student—such as, "I go to the public library to find answers to questions" or "I get great books at the library"—would be effective. Have the students hold up their library cards.
- Have a small reward, such as the reproducible doorknob hangers included in the handbook, for any student who shows you a library card.
- Have teachers, administrators, or volunteers stop students in the hall and ask if they have a library card. If they do, give them a small prize, such as a bite-sized candy bar, a sticker, or a bookmark.
- Let students make video book commercials. Broadcast during morning programs.

Copies of the handbook and posters also went to every public library in the state. Within the handbook was a section on the ways public libraries could promote Ticket to Read. The following ideas were included:

- Call media specialists in local schools and arrange to visit the schools.
- Arrange to talk briefly at a faculty meeting about the public library and its resources.
- Provide schools with specific information about your library's procedures for getting a library card. The brochure for students will tell them to bring parents and something with their address on it when they come to the library to get a library card.
- Sponsor a bookmark contest for children to draw a picture about a favorite book. Print copies of the winner to distribute in the library and in that child's school. You could also use a theme of "Why Kids Should Have a Library Card."
- Talk to at least one group (such as the PTA) about the importance of reading to children or encouraging children to read. Include information about why library cards are really a ticket to read.
- Give something to children who get their first library card. This can be as simple as a bookmark, a sticker, or a stamp on their hand. Encourage all staff to congratulate the child for getting a card.
- During the year, plan some family nights for various schools in your service area. If a school has a regular family night, see if the school would be willing to have it at the public library one night. If the school does not have family nights, ask if the school would be interested in cooperating for a special family night at the library. This would be a time to read stories, do a puppet show, talk about new books, give tours, and offer some other fun book-related activities.

The handbook, like the entire program, provides each school and public library with a foundation on which to plan its own library card campaign. What the state has done, using LSTA funding, is to lay the groundwork and develop an overall theme. Individual public and school libraries probably would not have the time, or the contacts, to do work with sponsors, organize public service announcements, and design graphics. By doing that work for every library, the South Carolina State Library and the South Carolina Association of School Librarians have given each library a jump start on getting every elementary-age child a ticket to read.

See the "Gallery of Successful Library Card Campaign Programs" for these documents from the South Carolina State Library:

√ McDonald's Tray Mat
√ Ticket to Read Poster
√ Ticket to Read Report Form
√ Ticket to Read Information Sheet

REFERENCE

Ticket to Read: Library Card Campaign for Elementary Schools in South Carolina. 2000. Columbia, S.C.: South Carolina State Library; South Carolina Association of School Librarians.

16 WHAT WORKS AND WHY: AN ALPHABET OF BEST PRACTICES FOR LIBRARY CARD CAMPAIGNS (CO-WRITTEN WITH ERICA KLEIN)

It became obvious in Houston Public Library's Power Card Challenge program that, in addition to changing the library's image for the customers outside of the library, the campaign itself was changing many things within the organization. In almost every campaign described in this book, even those in the small libraries, the absolute bottom-line factor in making every program work was the willingness to change. In some cases, like Houston Public Library, change represented a shift in thinking about the library and its role in the community. In other cases, the change was simply improving upon a policy or adding value to the already existing library card. But each library card campaign was, in and of itself, a change effort. To have a successful library card campaign is, in effect, to lead a successful change effort.

The library card campaigns outlined in this volume were each successful. Each library serves a distinct community so a campaign from one library cannot, and should not, be simply taken as a whole for use in another setting. It won't fit. Each library card campaign came about due to a certain set of circumstances, some of them not in the library's control. Without Mayor Brown, there would have been no Power Card. His election created the circumstances to create the campaign. Also, having new staff inside the library (such as a library director or youth services manager), or outside the library (such as a new school superintendent) played a role in many of these campaigns. One clear lesson is to seize moments such as these, or events such as switching library automation vendors. Some campaigns succeeded because of the cooperation of schools, some despite the lack of partnership. Some worked with little extra funding, others required and utilized funding from outside sources such as grant funds, corporate partners, library foundations, and Friends of the Library groups. Little attention is paid in this book to the cost of these campaigns, because the real decisions are not about allocating resources, but first about setting priorities. When a library system decides, for whatever reason (and plenty of good ones have been explored), to pursue a library card campaign, resources must be allocated toward the program for it to succeed. Even if outside resources are obtained, until the public and the staff see the campaign as a high priority, the campaign won't garner heavy attention.

Each library card campaign was successful because a variety of elements were present. What follows is an alphabetic summary of 26 of the best practices utilized in these library card campaigns. In addition to looking at the library aspect of these campaigns, in these best practices, the organizational dynamics will also be examined and discussed.

- **Appoint a project manager:** A library card campaign is lots of things, but mostly it is an example of a project involving different library staff and departments. It also involves a great deal of record keeping, networking, logistical work, and coordination. Primarily, especially in larger systems, it involves the planning and distribution of resources. A project manager who may or may not be a librarian can become the point person. Campaigns that involve outreach need someone to coordinate the campaign logistics, and sponsors need someone to serve as a liaison and to record their contributions. Campaigns involve ordering incentives, materials, and other supplies and someone needs to do that. While the "buck" stops with the director or the mayor, an operational person needs to see to the details.

  In the campaigns described, often the project manager was a person already on staff who was then given an extra set of duties. While obtaining new staff is difficult, more libraries should attempt to support a project manager position. The position could be flexible and used to manage a wide variety of projects, not just library card campaigns. Once "on the books," a project manager position could be moved from department to department, or from project to project. Imagine the success of long-range plans or other "big" initiatives (which sound good on paper, yet seldom reach their potential), if there were a person whose entire day-to-day job was the care and feeding of such an initiative.

- **<u>B</u>rand your library card:** Branding does several things, but it mainly serves to give the library a new image. By making new library cards and developing new materials around them, as with a product launch, the public may just come to view libraries in a whole new light. In Houston, the Power Card brand was everywhere. Every piece of paper that left the library's public information office carried the Power Card brand. The colors of the Power Card, in particular the bright orange, became the palette to build Web pages, reports, displays, and other documents. Branding also creates excitement: something very old and traditional like a library card suddenly becomes new when it transforms into a Power Card, a KNOWcard, or a WILD Card. Given the appeal of brands to children and teens, campaigns aimed at youth almost demand branding.

  Many of the campaigns created T-shirts for staff, for sale to the public, or for promotional incentives. While some staff members might resist wearing them, the T-shirts help create a spirit of community among library staff, reminding everyone they are all on the same team working toward the same goals. Out in the community, the T-shirts are used for outreach and to identify staff. Branding is another example of libraries looking to the commercial world for clues on how to improve their public image and expand their "market share." Library card campaigns are, at the most basic level, libraries attempting to get more people to buy their product—even if the product is free.

- **<u>C</u>ommitments from schools:** Almost every campaign described here involved working with schools. Most campaigns involved getting a commitment from the schools to support the program, but several, such as that of the Austin Public Library, took the extra step and made sure that commitment was made in writing and in public through a resolution from the school board. Some schools went further and cowrote with libraries letters that went directly to parents, thus linking the district and the superintendent to the program in the eyes of parents. Similarly, the process of asking staff to sign the banner at the final Power Card retreat also served the purpose of locking in their commitment. The postcards used in the Power Card campaign asked people to check a box stating, "Yes, my organization supports the Power Card Challenge" and then take an action (request applications) to back up that statement. An ideal campaign should include some way for schools to make a public commitment and perform visible actions supporting that commitment.

- **Define your vision and goals clearly:** Many of the campaigns described in this book began with a vision, often from a mayor who controls the library purse strings, to get every child a library card. From that vision, a plan emerges. A library card campaign of any size requires a plan that describes WHAT is going to be done, WHEN, by WHOM, and HOW. The WHY is the vision of the mayor, the initiative of the strategic plan, or the desire to network better in the community. The WHY needs to be clearly and persuasively articulated not just for the public, but also for a sometimes cynical staff who might see a library card campaign as just more work and more "hot air" from the library administration.

The WHAT should be goals that are difficult, yet attainable. They should be reasonable, measurable, and specific. The methods of counting success need to be figured out before the program begins, not halfway into it. For example, if one measure of success is an increase in the circulation of children's videos, by branch, then make sure there is a system in place that tracks at the necessary level. While the WHAT might be to get every child a card, that is not an attainable goal. Providing all children with an application to get a card is more attainable. Goals that are perceived to be unattainable are not motivating, and goals that are too easy are less motivating than challenging goals. Admonishments to "do your best" are also less motivating than challenging, specific goals.

Pilot programs, like that in Austin, should help set goals by delivering some hard data about what to expect in terms of both school cooperation and the number of students who will return applications. Even a library card sign-up goal that is measurable and seems relatively simple (for example, sign up 4,000 new youth borrowers) needs to be clearly defined. Does such a goal really mean entering 4,000 new applications, or does it mean a net gain of 4,000? That is, does the number represent the number of new registrations minus those cards that have expired, or just the number of new sign-ups? If there is a goal to increase circulation, does it mean an increase in circulation overall? Does it mean circulation by those with new cards? Does it mean increase the number of cards in use at the beginning of each month? How does one figure in changes in circulation when branches are closed or when a branch is in temporary facilities during a renovation? If the library card initiative is tied to a literacy campaign, should it only track increases in book circulation and not, for example, audio formats? If the campaign is about technology and the access that it provides, then there must be a way to measure technology usage before and after the campaign.

In addition to overall library goals, departments, branches, and units should have their own goals that are related to the overall goals. What specifically will the Central Library fine arts department do to support the library card goal? Within each department, individuals might have goals incorporated into yearly performance planning. The goals should be set, if possible, by each department/individual or cooperatively with each department/individual and the campaign leaders. While participating in goal setting has not been found to increase performance toward the goal, it has been found to increase commitment toward reaching the goal. Goal setting can thus help reduce cynicism by bringing more staff on board and can increase the duration of commitment past the initial spurt of enthusiasm.

- **Enable staff to be creative:** One of the great joys for those involved in the Power Card campaign was watching people flex their creative muscles—and not just the youth librarians. All across the system, staff members whose main jobs had been to check in or check out books were letting their creative juices flow, from writing Power Card poems to creating displays to thinking of new ideas for reaching out to the community. A library card campaign can become an idea machine, allowing people who don't always get a chance to contribute creatively to the organization a chance to do so. Campaign creativity may have another enduring benefit: to create a culture where creativity and innovation are nurtured, appreciated, and rewarded.

  "E" could also stand for "empower," although that is a loaded word that seems to have one set of meanings for staff and another set for management. If used incorrectly, "empowering" staff may lead to cynicism and resistance. Specify in what ways staff is empowered. Can staff break certain rules, in particular regarding registration or fines, in order to further the campaign? Can they bypass certain permissions and chains of command? If not, then how are they empowered?

- **Flexibility in working with schools:** For years public libraries have been attempting, not always with great success, to work with schools. Often the failure comes from a lack of understanding about what really happens in schools. Since schools know their pace, rhythms, and rules better than we ever could, libraries doing a library card campaign must be flexible in working with schools. The pitch should be made to the schools to participate, but let them decide the best way to go about it. One size does not fit all. Realize that the promotion and presentation of the campaign need to be different for first graders and tenth graders. While it may be more expensive, having two library card campaigns aimed at youth, one for elementary and one for secondary, may be the best strategy, as demonstrated by the successes in Birmingham and Portland.
- **Goals need to be tracked and information needs to be communicated:** Once goals have been set, staff and the public need to know how well the library is doing. Examples of good communication are the Power Tower at the Houston Public Library and the monthly Power Card reports which contained charts tracking progress toward the campaign's goals. In Philadelphia, each monthly meeting began with a review and discussion of the numbers and a review of what branches might need more assistance in reaching their goals.

  An important factor is not to wait until the end, or near the end, of the campaign, to share information about progress toward the goals. Throughout the campaign, staff need to be updated on the status of the campaign. This process allows staff an opportunity to change their strategy or redirect their efforts. While goals are not meant to be competitive, as normally they are part of a common overall goal, information about the progress of each branch or unit is equally important. If one branch is very successful, then branches that are running into resistance might want to inquire about success strategies. Also, this process would allow a system to reallocate resources. For example, if the one branch has most of its schools reaching 90 percent of their students, while the schools of another branch are reaching only 20 percent, then staff could be moved or shifted for short-term projects from a successful branch to one that has yet to achieve the same success.

  Finally, success toward reaching goals needs to be determined by a variety of metrics, not simply a raw number of sign-ups. When appropriate, goals need to be measured using ratios and percentages. In this way, small agencies are not seen as "penalized" because they signed up only 100 students during a month while a larger branch with more staff might have signed up 1,000. (Consider, too, that a branch that even before a library card campaign has always been very successful at working with schools may have fewer sign-ups only because the community is already loaded with library cards.) Regardless of the metric, staff always need to know where they stand toward meeting system goals.

- **High touch and high tech:** In just about every campaign described in this book it was typically not a flyer or a poster that motivated a young person to sign up for a library card; it was a visit. While very staff-intensive, the "high touch" aspect of library card campaigns is the key to their success. Not only does a visit serve to rally youth to sign up for cards, it also gives students a "face" to recognize again in the library. School visits help further the partnerships between librarians and teachers. Each visit can become an invitation for another visit or another extension of the library's service to students. Use the opportunity to put those "assignment alert" forms into teachers' hands when you are in their classroom. Use this opportunity to hand out information about "old school" library services, such as tours or booktalking, as well as information about databases, Internet access, and information literacy activities.

  High technology has been the focus on several campaigns—it provides the public with a "new" reason to get a library card. The Los Angeles Public Library used the slogan "Books are only the beginning" while the Durham County Library tied the library card campaign to a technology push. Technology has pushed many library systems to issue new cards, and thus technology creates the opportunity for a library card campaign.

- **Involve youth and other volunteers:** Among all of these campaigns, perhaps the most noteworthy single activity was the Austin Public Library's contest to design the Star Card, which was won by a twelve-year-old. This is powerful youth involvement that not only rewards the students who win but also demonstrates the library's commitment to involving and valuing youth. Student volunteers were involved in several campaigns, bringing energy and also creating hype. The design of that hype, in particular among high schoolers, should be left to the students themselves through youth advisory groups like those in Multnomah County. Since high schools have been the most difficult of the youth audiences to reach in just about every campaign, involving youth in the planning and even the implementation of campaigns at their schools is a must. If organizations like the National Honor Society need to earn community service points, why not suggest having members help the library with a library card campaign? Teens could also be trained to help the library with outreach on the weekends or evenings.

Many campaigns could not have taken place without the work of volunteers, who did everything from stuffing envelopes to preparing campaign packets. Volunteers play a huge role in successful library card campaigns. Some campaigns involved training volunteers in actually doing the library card registration. The most powerful use of volunteers involved service organizations or other organized groups looking for community service projects, such as the Evanston Public Library's involvement of PTA members in helping with sign-ups at schools.

- **Join forces with a local corporation or retailer:** While the Houston Public Library could possibly have done a successful library card campaign without the backing of Reliant Energy, it would have been much more difficult. Reliant provided the library with expertise and also served as a key player in some of the most important aspects of the campaign, namely developing incentives and rewards. Reliant bought pizza one year and popcorn the next for the entire staff, and contributed to other staff morale boosters as well. Even more important was Reliant's sponsorship of the school banner program. Furthermore, Reliant's support was not only a matter of having more funding but of having private funding. Most libraries, as public institutions, navigate a maze to purchase materials other than books. While obtaining bids and working through the rest of the process are standard library operating procedure, in the Power Card Challenge funding was sometimes needed for immediate projects such as printing press kits. For Reliant, an important benefit was the instant recognition and positive public relations the project brought to the company's name. Reliant was able to leverage suppliers and partners to help the library. Almost all of the campaigns described in this book involved seeking donations and/or sponsorships because private companies can bring more clout and cash to the table than any public library.

One of the keys to corporate sponsorship is finding a business with a track record of supporting literacy efforts in the community, or at least a history of working with the library. The corporate partners also need to learn what "they get" out of participating in such a campaign. While different levels of sponsors were developed for the Power Card, most major partners received credit in press releases, reports, and documents, and during press events. Reliant, as the title sponsor, got their logo on just about every item that contained the Power Card logo. But equally important is a real involvement of the partner. The people at Reliant didn't just share their money with the Houston Public Library; they truly shared in the success of the campaign. A Reliant representative was often invited to attend Power Card steering committee meetings, and was regularly briefed via e-mail on the status of the project. Reliant participated in the Public Library Association program about the Power Card in Charlotte, and sent representatives to local events, such as banner giveaways.

- **Keep good records:** By the end of the program, you should have an excellent database of contacts: teachers, community leaders, and others who have been part of the program. To gather statistics and track the success of the program, and to ensure that you can get the numbers and reports you need, get information technology people on board early. Get breakdowns of sign-ups or circulation or other measures of success by location, by age, or whatever other numbers you think would help you evaluate how well and where the campaign is working. With such data you can make better decisions. For example, during the final year of the Power Card campaign, it was decided to place billboards around town again, this time with a new slogan, "Get it! Got it? Use it!" The billboards were placed strategically near only those branch libraries which were still reporting low sign-ups. This approach could not have been used without accurate records of success metrics, by branch.

Chicago Public and other campaigns developed excellent reporting forms to make the tracking information easier to manage. For the Power Card, each branch was asked during one year to complete an outreach log documenting where they went out into the community, how successful the visit was in terms of registration, and the amount of staffing that was required for each event

But as important as all the numbers are, perhaps even more important are collecting success stories that go hand-in-hand with library card campaigns. Many more private and public funders are looking for libraries to produce outcomes and document the impact of our work. Library card campaigns provide examples to document the good work we do serving the public and partnering in the community. Yet, as important as numbers and words are, there is something about a picture of a young child holding up a library card. The Power Card Challenge was, thanks to the advent of digital cameras and scanners, very well documented in photos. Some photos were used for media kits and some were used in the library's annual report. Some branches took their own photos of kids holding up their new cards, either at an outreach event or when the children came into the branch library. The reason to keep good records is not only to be able to document what has been done and to prove its success, but also to create memories, which pictures (and video) do quite well.

- **Library media specialists are the first, but not the only, partners:** In any library card campaign involving schools, the school librarians should be the first contact but not the only contact. Within schools are other key individuals, such as the supervisor of the reading department, who need to be brought on board. School departments related to volunteers, curriculum development, parent education, parent organizations, and community partners should be contacted and asked to partner. At the upper grade levels it is important to get coaches and club sponsors involved as well as faculty.

  That said, almost every single library card drive described in this book was successful because of the role played by the school media specialist. In the campaigns that are almost entirely school-based, like the Chicago campaign, the media specialist might seem, for the life of the sign-up drive, almost like a public library staff member. In addition to the fact that the intense involvement of the school media specialist shows support for student achievement, there are so many benefits for the program. The public gets to see schools and city departments working together for the good of their kids, which is a nice message for both institutions to send. Libraries fulfill the partnership initiatives deemed so important by the "bible" of school library media programs, *Information Power*. But mostly what the library card campaign can do for both the school and public librarian is develop a relationship through one project which can lead to other projects in the future. Many of the campaigns discussed in this book included incentives not only for students to participate, but also for teachers and the school librarians.

- **Morale matters:** If the key to success in most campaigns is the staff, then staff resistance can certainly be one of the elements of failure. Poor morale often emerges out of employee cynicism. Cynicism in the workplace has two components: first, the belief that things can improve, and second the belief that things will not improve given the current management and strategies. Cynicism is increased by failed initiatives and projects. The very nature of cynicism suggests that the most cynical staff members might actually be optimists: they believe things can be better, but the current direction of the library isn't making the necessary improvements. If those people can be identified and brought on board to help in planning, implementing, and evaluating the campaign, other staff might then think, for example, "Boy, if Patrick thinks this can work, then it must really be a good plan."

Since a library card campaign is going to change the nature of how libraries operate, the staff element always needs to be at the forefront. Training is important: many people might not want to take on more simply because they don't feel they can do a good job. Also, staff members need to know what resources are available to them so they don't feel they are being asked to do more with less. The obvious but sometimes ignored rule, then, is: Don't ask staff to do more if they don't have enough resources. Find tradeoffs that do not sacrifice customer service and that will enable more resources to be dedicated toward the campaign. For example, can volunteers take on more clerical work and in doing so allow paid staff to spend more time doing direct customer service?

One reason, perhaps, to involve volunteers in outreach is because not all library staff feel comfortable going out in the community, and, because of family considerations, not all are able to adjust their schedules to do outreach. Some staff may not be able to work outside, while others may not have transportation. Some, such as the facilities management staff, catalogers, IT support personnel, or shelvers may not be trained in processing applications or even in interacting with customers. That does not mean such staff do not contribute to successful campaigns. They support the campaigns by doing their everyday tasks or by staying "on the desk" while librarians who love outreach dive headlong into another event or school event. Library card campaigns aimed at youth create more work for everyone, not just children's librarians. Because of that, everyone should be involved in some level since everyone has a stake in the success of the campaign. Libraries must take time to recognize the delivery drivers who move books around the system so kids can check them out, the IT people who repair the computers so applications can be processed, and the people in cataloging and processing who move materials from boxes to library shelves. The morale of the people behind the scenes is just as important as that of those in public services.

- **Network in the community and let the community get involved:** So many of the campaigns described in this book involved not just schools and a corporate sponsor, but many people from the community. Few people are going to be against children getting library cards. Neighborhood associations, parent-teacher groups, educational organizations, and the youth collaborative are starting points. The campaign in Des Moines grew out of the library's work in the youth collaborative, while many of the contacts that supported the Houston Power Card campaign came from networking that was done before the campaign even started. Every conversation with a community contact should end with asking if the person can recommend three other people who might support the project.

- **Offer amnesty days:** A successful technique used in several campaigns was the decision not only to waive the fee for a replacement card during the sign-up period (which just makes so much sense), but also to waive previous fines. Missoula's "Food for Fido" campaign is a creative twist on that approach. Fines are tricky things and amnesty may not, given the politics and levels where such decisions are made, be practical. However, it sends a good message to the community and also removes obstacles for kids reregistering for cards. The fines most of these kids owe will never be collected anyway. Thus, the fine doesn't really serve its real purpose, which is to increase access to the collection. But if fines prohibit young people from getting cards during a card campaign, then the fine is self-defeating; it is denying access, not increasing it.

- **P̲olitical support is a must:** Many of these campaigns described in this book began with a politician wanting to see something happen and many of the campaigns maintained some visibility in the community because of the continued support of a politician (or, in some cases, a politician's spouse). Thus, the very first person to sell on doing a library card campaign is whoever holds the purse strings to funding the library, not only because a campaign will cost money and will require more resources, but also because political support is crucial to the strength of the campaign. But that is only the beginning, as council members or county commissioners also need to be brought on board. Library cards for kids is not exactly a controversial stand. One of the best pictures of the entire Power Card campaign is that of the Houston City Council standing with the mayor and the library director all showing off their Power Cards. An even better picture came about a year later when two council members on totally opposite sides of the political spectrum, who rarely worked together on anything and even rarely agreed on any issue, came together to help the library celebrate Read Across America Day. Support of reading creates strange political bedfellows, which can only serve us to our advantage.
- **Q̲uestion everything:** Why do we fine youth materials? Why do we require a parent signature? Why do we limit the number of items a patron can check out in some formats and not others? Why does one format have a different check-out period and fine rate from another? Library card campaigns are the perfect opportunity to ask basic questions about every aspect of library services, in particular relating to youth use and circulation policies.
- **R̲eward staff, sponsors, and teachers:** Every library card campaign outlined in this book had incentives built into it. Some were donated, some were purchased, and some were free, but all demonstrated that getting people to change their behavior works a lot better with a carrot (or cake) than it does with a stick. The banners used in the Power Card campaign worked as rewards for schools and their principals even if they did nothing directly for students. Other campaigns, like that in Phoenix, were loaded with incentives not only for getting a card, but also for using it. The Philadelphia program built in an incentive for the teen staff who garnered the most registrations. Almost all campaigns included incentives for teachers and school librarians who participated, with more for those who got all of the students signed up.

The Power Card program was greatly concerned with rewarding staff with programs like the Polo Club and the Blue Crew. Yet, the staff survey showed that the very programs that the administration thought would reward (and thus motivate) staff were, in fact, the most controversial and most hated. Why reward a few people when everyone works hard? That seemed to be the common complaint, yet if you reward everyone, is it really a reward? The right answer is to listen to your staff and to see what works in your system. Don't get stubbornly locked into a reward plan that isn't well received. Exhibit some flexibility. Try asking staff to design a reward program and see what they come up with. Consider the implications of reward programs that set up competitive situations among individuals and groups, where one must win and the others by default lose, versus reward programs where everyone who is doing well can be rewarded. Both methods have advantages and disadvantages—choose what works for your people.

It is important to realize that people differ in what they consider a reward and that they differ in the extent to which they enjoy public recognition—some find it embarrassing and even unpleasant, while others love it. Thus, rewards need to be varied and flexible, and they must not be postponed until the end of the program. The concept of catching people doing things right is always a good one in libraries, never more so than in a library card campaign when lots of people are doing lots of "right" things. If praise is genuine, then you cannot give "too much" praise.

- **Share information about the program widely, internally and externally:** The key here is to use multiple channels. Most of the card campaigns described in this book involved some sort of media partnership to make sure that people learned about the campaign in different ways. While all media partnerships are important, perhaps the daily newspaper is the most vital. Given their desire to have young people become readers and thus future newspaper customers, they are nearly perfect partners. Several of the campaigns, like those in Austin and Philadelphia, received not just excellent editorial coverage, but also were given free space to promote the campaign.

Internally, multiple channels need to be used. Just sending a memo isn't sufficient, since people take in information in so many different ways. Some people prefer to read it, others to hear it. Some even need to see it. One technique that worked with some success in the Power Card campaign was a Power Card notebook. Bright orange, three-ring notebooks were sent to every library department. All reports, memos, or documents about the Power Card were already three-hole punched and they often came with a reminder to the manager to put the information in the notebook and to share the information in individual and group meetings.

- **Target your campaign:** The library card campaign in Philadelphia serves as the perfect example of realizing that you can overextend your resources by trying to reach everyone and then actually end up reaching fewer people. The most successful campaigns seem to be those that focused on specific grades, with grades K–2 seemingly the most popular. A better approach used by some campaigns is to focus on transition grades where students might be entering a new school. This method makes sense because new students in a new school require new paperwork, one piece of which can be a library card application. Since most library cards expire after a few years, this approach will ensure that students are getting the opportunity to be re-registered and are reminded of the importance of libraries.

- **Understand obstacles:** The Austin campaign began by asking the right question: not "How can we convince people to have cards?" but rather "What is preventing people from getting cards?" Those obstacles might be ignorance of procedures, inconvenience or perceived inconvenience, or perhaps lack of awareness of library services and availability. In Des Moines the question wasn't "Why don't we do more programs for youth in the summer?" but rather "Why don't more kids attend the programs we do offer?" The obstacle was transportation, so that became the focus of the campaign. In Phoenix, transportation also became an issue for getting the first graders to use their cards, so the library worked with the transit authority to make it easy for teachers to arrange tours and class visits using the city bus system for free.

- **Value added to the library card:** Many successful campaigns described in this book involved getting local merchants or cultural organizations to offer discounts or other perks for getting or showing a library card. We know that library cards are valuable in and of themselves, but adding value to the card not only acts as another incentive, it also shows the library being active in the community.

Those partnerships we have in place for summer reading could be expanded to include library card campaigns. South Carolina's program offered free admission to college baseball games and the Power Card's program offered discounted admission to the Johnson Space Center tourist attraction.

- **Wise up—learn from the successes and challenges of other campaigns (and your own):** This book is a start. You can also find information about current campaigns in library journals and newspapers. Libraries are not like cable companies; they are generally not in competition with one another. You'll find that people in other systems are often very generous about sharing ideas and experiences, as they were with the author. Few of the campaigns described in this book were written up in the library literature before appearing in this publication. In addition, for every campaign described in this book there are also similar and just as successful campaigns occurring that are known only to the few staff working on them, and the community benefiting from the project. If you are doing a campaign, let everyone know about it through a listserv, a publication, applying for (and winning) awards, as well as by presenting the campaign results at a state conference.

In many of these campaigns, it was noted how the library changed processes or procedures in midstream. In Philadelphia, for example, they learned that a targeted campaign worked best. In Houston, by holding retreats, distributing surveys, and encouraging lots of communication about the Power Card program, the library learned about both the program's successes and failures. Quarterly, the steering committee would bring together the chairs of the work teams to hash out issues, and then the chairs would go meet among themselves to share ideas.

The Power Card Web page is another example of trying to create a "learning organization" that shared information and ideas rapidly. At the Central Library in Houston, the shared drive contained a "cards" folder which anyone involved in the campaign could access to find a document. Very little work was done more than once: letters for one purpose were modified for another. Mailing lists were created and then stored for later use. In many of the campaigns described in this book, so much of the success emerged not from fancy cards, but from conversations between management and staff, and between people at different levels of the organization about ways to improve the campaign.

- **eXit the library and get out into the community:** The amount of outreach generated by library card campaigns is reason enough to undertake them. There are only two ways to increase the use of any public library: get the people already using it to use it more, or get more people to use it. The way to do that is through promotion, and community outreach is the best promotion since it allows us to tell our story persuasively, demonstrably, and in person. The library card campaign in Prince George's County used a van traveling around the county to attend events like baseball games and concerts. The focus was on visiting places where people congregated. Outreach not only gets people signed up for cards, it sends a very strong message to the community about the involvement of the public library.

- **Youth first:** Some of the campaigns described in this book were general in nature, and even a few were aimed at adults, but most focused on youth. They focused on youth not only because it made sense politically, but also because focusing on youth seems to be a smart way for libraries to proceed to build their base. Almost every child has a parent. Thus, by focusing on youth, the library is really targeting families. During the Power Card Challenge, adult circulation and adult registration climbed right along with youth figures, although not at the same clip. Why? Two reasons. First, in order to use these new cards they were getting at schools or through Scouts or through some other venue, children would need their parents to accompany them to the library. For many parents, it was their first trip to a library in years. By motivating the child, the parent followed. But equally as important, the overall campaign increased the visibility of the library in the community, so even people without children knew and cared about the Power Card.

  Library card campaigns for youth are also easier than campaigns for adults. Working through schools, libraries have access to children and teens in large groups. Large groups of adults are harder to reach (save those campaigns which had successful sign-up campaigns at work places). Within schools, through teachers and school librarians, there are other adults who are willing, able, and even eager to help the library fulfill goals for getting kids signed up for cards.

  Only a few campaigns, the WILD Card from Birmingham and the KewlCard from Multnomah County, focused just on getting library cards into the hands of teenagers. Both of the campaigns were quite successful. High school students were the hardest audience to reach during the Power Card campaign—because time is so tight at the secondary level and because teachers and students are more distracted with other activities. They are also a harder sell, but that does not mean it is not worth it. If anything, while library card campaigns for babies and preschoolers generate good press and wonderful photos, library card campaigns should have some focus on the upper grades. These are the students who most need cards to check out books to complete homework, to access databases for research, to find materials to read for pleasure, and to find information for the important "life work" they are undertaking. Working closely with teachers who assign research, with coaches and club sponsors, as well as with parent groups, in addition to offering incentives (food never hurts) seem to be keys to success.

If Mayor Brown had said he wanted every adult in the city to research his or her family history, then the Houston Public Library probably would have done the Family Tree Trial to make sure everyone visited the Clayton Genealogy Library. But that was not his vision, nor is it the goal of most mayors. In most cities, city government does have direct control over the schools, thus the mayor and council members who want to be pro-education and pro-youth need only look toward public libraries where the majority of users are under the age of 18. Library card campaigns focusing on youth let libraries operate to the strongest potential market, the one most likely to garner political support, and the one that brings to the library the energy that only youth services can provide.

- **Zzz, libraries are boring—NOT; make it fun:** Assumption: most people—including staff and our customers—want to be part of something that is fun. A memorable Power Card story is that of the tough-as-nails eighth grader at Key Middle School proudly showing off his Power Card to a friend and saying, "You know, you can use this at any library in Houston." From the Power Card raps to the Power Card Wheel to Power Card dress-up days, one of the overriding goals of the program was to make the library fun. Fun for kids to use, fun for parents to visit, and fun for staff to come to each morning. Staff want to be part of a winning team and they want to be part of things that are successful. Over and over again in all these campaigns, the success doesn't come down to just these 26 "best practices" but really just to one: staff participation.

The various best practices here focus on staff and organizational concerns, like communication, empowerment, morale, and positive reinforcement, for good reason. All staff, not just the children's librarians, are what make library card campaigns happen. Staff members who reach not just out into the community, but down within themselves to come up with new ideas and a new way of looking at things. Campaigns to get more people library cards are just as much about getting staff more involved and engaged in their work. The success is measured in numbers of cards, but it is also measured in impact and outcomes. It is measured by kids running into libraries and getting new cards or posing for pictures with those new cards. It is measured by more books and videos flying off the shelves. It is measured by more people knowing exactly what it is that public libraries do. Finally, what library card campaigns do is quite basic. This free item brings value. When kids have cards, they have access to information. They are empowered and they are on a path toward healthy youth development. A community which values youth will support programs like library card campaigns because it supports healthy youth development. For all the costs of promoting and issuing these free passes to information, the payoff is tremendous. In fact, it is downright powerful.

GALLERY OF SUCCESSFUL LIBRARY CARD CAMPAIGN PROGRAMS

Documents in the appendix of this book were reprinted with permission. All documents retain copyright of the original creators and should not be reproduced without written consent.

Houston Public Library   Power Card Application (English)
             Power Card Application (Spanish)
             Power Card Report
             Power Card Express
             Pack the Power Brochure
             Power Card Postcard

Chicago Public Library   Library Card Rap
             Receipt for Library Cards
             Form for Incomplete or Unsuccessful Application

Los Angeles Public Library Sign of Intelligent Life in LA Brochure/Application

San Jose Public Library   Wild About Reading Application Return Form
             Wild About Reading Application

Multnomah County Public Library
             Get Carded! Poster
             Great Library Card Adventure Poster
             Great Library Card Adventure Instructions for Teachers
             Get Carded! Instruction for Teachers
             Great Library Card Adventure Postcard for Kindergarten
             Great Library Card Adventure Kit Information

Austin Public Library   Star Card Flyer
             Star Card Application
             Star Card "Dear Parent or Guardian" Letter

Birmingham Public Library and Jefferson County Library Cooperative	WILD Card Application Licensed to Read Application Licensed to Read Poster
Durham County Public Library	Technology Open House Invitation Get Connected to the World Bookmark
Jefferson County Public Library	Sign Up Today Application
New Orleans Public Library	Kids Club Newsletter Kids Club Application
Phoenix Public Library	Congratulations Brochure Project GOAL Poster Project GOAL Classroom Poster
Pikes Peak Library District	Just Say "Yes" to the KNOWcard Brochure KNOW What Brochure KNOW the Power Brochure KNOWcard Teacher Letter KNOWcard Tally Sheet KNOWcard Registration Process for Schools Flyer KNOWcard Letter to Parents KNOWcard Fact Sheet Inform, Empower, Inspire Flyer
Richmond Public Library	Happy Birthday Flyer
Fountaindale Public Library	Battle of the Books Flyer
Missoula Public Library	Proclamation Food for Fido Flyer Winning Contest Entries
Putnam County Public Library	Dear Parent Letter

Washington-Centerville
Public Library   Program Flyer

South Carolina State
Library   McDonald's Tray Mat
                                      Ticket to Read Poster
                                      Ticket to Read Report Form
                                      Ticket to Read Information Sheet

Go to any branch of the
Houston Public Library to get your own *Power* Card™ and you'll discover
everything from the ABC's to the SAT's.

Books · Comic Books and Magazines · Paperbacks · Music CDs, Audio Tapes and Videos

PLUS!

The Internet · Homework help · Programs for all ages

Find out more at **www.hpl.lib.tx.us**

- ✂ - - -

◼ **Yes, I believe that knowledge is power. I'm ready to get my *Power* Card™ at a Houston Public Library.**

(Please print in blue or black ink and take this flyer to any Houston Public Library.)

Student's Name _____   Student's Date of Birth ___ / ___ / ___
                First   Middle   Last

Address _____   City/State/Zip _____

Parent/Guardian's Name _____   Telephone (day) _____

Parent/Guardian Driver's License or Texas I.D. # _____   (evening) _____

                                      E-mail _____

                                      **(for circulation notices and
Library information)**

*Note to Parents: *I understand that I am responsible for the use of this card including any fines or fees, and for my child's selection
of materials and use of electronic resources, including the Internet.*

22 447 ___ ___   ___ ___ ___   ___ ___ ___

             (for staff use only)

Corporate Sponsor

Reliant *Energy*™   _____

                                 Parent/Guardian's Signature *

Houston Public Library/Power Card Application (English)

Ve a cualquiera de las Bibliotecas

Públicas de Houston y obten tu propia Power **Card™ y descubriras la**

respuesta a todo, desde el ABC's hasta los SAT's.

Libros de todo tipo - Revistas - Revistas cómicas - Discos compactos - Videos - Cassettes

ADEMAS!

El Internet - Ayuda con tus tareas escolares - Programas para todas las edades

Para mayores informes consulta el **www. hpl.lib.tx.us en la computadora**

- ✂ - - -

■ Sí, yo creo que los conocimientos son el poder y estoy lista/o para recoger mi Power Card™ en la Biblioteca Pública de Houston.

(Por favor imprime en tinta azul o negra y lleva esta hoja a cualquier Biblioteca Pública de Houston.)

Nombre del Estudiante _____   **Fecha de Nacimiento** _____ / ___ / _____
                        Nombre   inicial   apellido

Dirección_____

Padres/Guardianes_____   **Teléfono (dia)** _____

Número de licencia de conducir de los padres o guardianes_____   **(noche)** _____

                                                        E-mail _____
                                                        (para anunciios de circulación
                                                        e información sobre la Biblioteca)

*Nota para los padres: *Comprendo que yo me hago responsable de la manera en que mis hijos usen esta tarjeta, incluyendo multas y otros costos; asi como de los materiales que mis hijos seleccionen y del uso que hagan de los recursos electrónicos, incluyendo el Internet.*

22 447   __ __ __   __ __ __   __ __ __
                    (sólo para uso del personal)
Patrocinador Corporativo

\\Reliant
Energy™   _____
                                              Firma de los padres o guardianes*

Houston Public Library/Power Card Application (Spanish)

DRESS UP
DAZE
Last Week Of
Each Month

POWER CARD REPORT

JUNE 2001

Monthly report on the Power Card Challenge

High Impact Squad Pushing the Power

The High Impact Squad mesmerized kids with there explosive and energetic performance. Lon LeMaster from Vinson branch said; They really supported reading and the Summer Reading program. This is a great way to win over a principal. Invite a principal to a High Impact Squad performance at a neighboring school whom you would like to impress and just sit back and watch. Jealousy is a w o n d e r f u l thing; We give all the credit to the C a r n e g i e Grant fund!

We have 3,118 to go!

TRACKING THE REGISTRATION GOAL

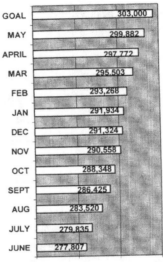

GOAL	303,000	
MAY	299,882	
APRIL	297,772	
MAR	295,503	
FEB	293,268	
JAN	291,934	
DEC	291,324	
NOV	290,558	
OCT	288,348	
SEPT	286,425	
AUG	283,520	
JULY	279,835	
JUNE	277,807	

260,000 275,000 290,000 305,000

	P C C	OUTREACH	EVENTS
June 21		Science and Health Museum	Gail Hicks
June 24		Children's Museum	Gail Hicks
July 22		Festival Traders Village	Gail Hicks

CIRCULATION
YTD THRU May 2001
2,905,902

GOAL FOR FY01
3,242,386*

% GOAL REACHED 89%

Average of total youth borrowers with items checked out for May is 45,055. That's an increase of 1,831 over the average for April.

The circulation goal reflects goal for total youth circulation. This equals juvenile circulation **plus young adult circulation*

Houston Public Library/Power Card Express (outside)

SPECIAL EDITION   HOUSTON, TEXAS   SEPTEMBER 2000

Mayor Brown named Library Journal Politician of the Year for his support of the Houston Public Library.

Staff Quotes

"The Library is more **kid focused."**

"The Library is more **visible."**

"The Library has more **vigor."**

The High "Impact" Squad packing the Power.

Outreach Highlights

- Baby & Child Expo
- Houston International Festival
- Museum District Day
- Healthy Kids Day
- Houston Children's Festival
- Battleship Texas Christmas
- Houston Livestock Show & Rodeo
- Southeast Texas Home School Association
- Fundays in the Park

Houston Public Library Pops the Top Off Power Card Challenge

⟶ Registration/Circulation

The Houston Public Library now has 277,807 active juvenile cardholders as of June 30, 2000, surpassing the goal of 240,000. Circulation of juvenile materials increased by 10% over the previous year. The success of the Power Card Challenge is due to Mayor Lee P. Brown's vision and the dynamic momentum created by the many Power Card programs, staff dedication and creativity, corporate and community support, school participation and support from the City of Houston.

Plenty stopped by the Power Card booth to sign-up.

Power Plus Programs

These programs were designed to give value-added benefits to Power Card holders.

- **The Children's Museum of Houston** Three free Sundays, one in May, June and July, 2000 gave Power Card holders two free admissions.
- **Museum of Fine Arts, Houston** Free admission for children 18 years and under every Saturday and Sunday throughout the year.

⟶ Powerful Awards

- 1999 Project of the Year, Texas Library Association
- First Place Bronze Quill Award for Illustration International Association of Business Communicators (IABC)
- "Best Government Giveaway," Houston Press "Best of 1999"
- 2000 John Cotton Dana Library Public Relations Award, American Library Association

"Our School Packs the Power" banner was presented to HISD 8th Ave. Elementary for having more than 90 percent of their students sign-up for a Houston Public Library Power card.

Goals for Fiscal Year 2000–2001

- Increase the number of juvenile cardholders to 303,000
- Increase the circulation of juvenile materials to 2,960,000 items by June 30, 2001
- Increase the number of juvenile borrowers with items checked out to 45,000 monthly.

Alison Landers, Assistant Director of Public Services (center), joins Power Card Region Team Leaders Mary Hammond, Andeberhan Tensae and Karen Vargas (to the left of Alison), Gail Hicks, Marilyn Ming, Hellena Stokes, and Karen Luik (to the left of Alison). Bill Coxsey moves the Power Critter up the "Tower of Power" to mark the goal of 240,000 juvenile cardholders, which was reached in less than half the time expected. Note the snappy new denim Power Shirts, given to those who make extraordinary efforts in support of the Power Card Challenge.

Houston Public Library/Power Card Express (inside)

How Do I Get a Power Card?

Apply in person at any Houston Public Library location for the Power Card—your library card. Library cards are free to City of Houston residents and the non-resident fee is waived for anyone residing in Harris County or the contiguous counties: Brazoria, Chambers, Fort Bend, Galveston, Liberty, Montgomery and Waller. Non-residents outside the eight county area may purchase a card for $40 a year or $20 for six months.

Registrations expire after three years, at which time they may be renewed. Children under 18 may get their own library cards with applications signed by parents or guardians. The parent or guardian must agree to be responsible for the use of the child's card including any fines or fees, and for the child's selection of materials and use of electronic resources, including the Internet.

What Kind of ID is Accepted When Applying?

As proof of residence, the Library accepts a Texas driver's license or Texas ID, utility or telephone bill, or a personalized check. If these are not available, please ask a staff member about alternate ID.

How Do I Renew My Power Card?

When your Power Card is near expiration, stop by the Central Library or any branch with your ID as noted above. Staff will verify your address and update the borrower record to reflect any changes. Any balance pending on the card must be paid prior to renewal. Resident and non-resident waiver cards are renewed for three years; non-resident cards are renewed for six or twelve months.

How Many Items May I Borrow?

In most cases, you may borrow as many items at one time as you like. Exceptions: you may not have more than 8 videos, 10 compact discs, and 2 CD-ROMs checked out on your card.

Online Access

Your Power Card is your passport to many valuable subscription databases that can be accessed for free by library cardholders, in addition to the world of service and information available through the Library's Web site. All Library locations offer access to the Internet on public workstations, but good judgement must be exercised. Parents and guardians must be responsible for their children's use of the Library's electronic resources, the Internet, and print and audiovisual materials. The Library provides computer workstations with filtering software in all libraries as an option for parents and guardians.

What If I Lose My Library Card?

If you lose your Power Card, a replacement card will cost $1. Report your lost or stolen library card to the Library as soon as possible to prevent others from charging materials to your account. You are responsible for all items charged to your card until its loss is reported.

How Long May I Keep Library Materials?

The usual loan period is two weeks, except for some audiovisual materials. Most items may be renewed twice for two-week periods each time at any library location. The maximum loan period, including renewal, is six weeks. Videos are loaned for 1 week with no renewals.

How Do I Renew Materials?

Customer self-renewal is available through eServices Personal Account Information and Renewal. You may also renew by e-mail, click on eServices, then E-mail Renewal from the Library's home page:

http://www.houstonlibrary.org

You may renew items in person at the Central Library or any branch. You may renew by phone by calling the Library's 24-hour renewal line (713-247-2280), or by calling any branch library during their operating hours.

You must have your library card number to renew by phone or email. Items for which renewal is requested will be renewed for two weeks from the date of renewal. Some items may not be eligible for renewal.

Where Do I Return My Borrowed Items?

All borrowed items may be returned to any Houston Public Library location. Films, videos and other audiovisual materials are relatively fragile and may not be placed in the book drop.

How Much Are Overdue Fines?

Fines for most adult and young adult items are 20 cents per day and 10 cents per day for most children's items. Fines for videos are $1 per day per item. Library cards may not be used when fines/fees reach $10. Library cards are activated again upon payment of the amount due. Fines and fees are established by the Houston City Council and are non-refundable.

Will the Library Hold Something for Me That Wasn't on the Shelf When I Looked?

Yes. For a non-refundable fee of $1 per item, the Library will attempt to locate a circulating item that is unavailable at the time of request. Reserve requests may be made in person or by mail, but not by phone.

What If I Lose Something I Borrow?

If library material is not returned within six weeks of the due date, you will receive a billing notice from the Library. In addition to the cost of the lost material, you will be charged a $10 non-refundable processing fee for each catalogued item, or a $5 non-refundable partial processing fee for each uncataloged item that is lost, plus any outstanding overdue fines. The same charges apply to items returned with serious damage.

For questions or concerns regarding circulation of library materials, please call:

HOUSTON PUBLIC LIBRARY
CIRCULATION DEPARTMENT
713-247-2222

is the Title Sponsor of the Power Card

Houston Public Library/Pack the Power Brochure

HOUSTON PUBLIC LIBRARY
500 McKinney
Houston, TX 77002
http://www.hpl.lib.tx.us

Gail Hicks
Power Card Project Manager
Houston Public Library
500 McKinney
Houston TX 77002

PowerCard PowerCard PowerCard PowerCard

☐ **YES,** I want my organization to be part of the *Power* Card° Challenge!

Send _____ **Power Card Challenge Applications to:**

_____

_____

_____

_____

Reliant Energy.
HL&P Entex

Contact me regarding Power Card Sign-Ups:

e-mail _____ **telephone** _____

For more information, contact Gail Hicks • 713-247-2224
ghicks@hpl.lib.tx.us • http://www.hpl.lib.tx.us/powercard

*The Power Card Challenge is a program of Mayor Lee P. Brown,
the City of Houston, and the Houston Public Library*

Houston Public Library/Power Card Postcard

LIBRARY CARD CAMPAIGN RAP

Want to make the team?
It isn't very hard.
All that you need
Is a library card!

Take home a form.
Did you know the card is free?
But be sure to fill the form out
CARE-FUL-LY.

Free! Free! The card is free!
The greatest bargain is your LI-BRARY!

Complete every line,
And what do you think?
Pencils no good.
You've gotta' use ink!

Have a parent sign it.
Now what to do?
Look for the line
Where YOU sign it, too!

Young and old, you and me!
Everybody's welcome at the LI-BRARY!

Hey! Now you've got your card.
Want to know the score:
You can take out books
And a whole lot more!

Programs, magazines, friends to see!
They've got it all at the LI-BRARY!

Chicago Public Library/Library Card Rap

CHICAGO PUBLIC LIBRARY/ CHICAGO PUBLIC SCHOOLS
RECEIPT FOR LIBRARY CARDS (Copy as Needed)

School_____   CPS representative_____
Phone Number_____   Fax #_____
Library_____   CPL contact person_____
Phone Number_____   Fax #_____

Library Cards Summary

Classroom #	Applications received	Cards Issued	Applications returned-incomplete	Applications returned-blocked record

Total Number of Library Applications dropped off at CPL_____
Total Number of Library Cards Issued from CPL_____
Total Number of Applications returned because incomplete._____
Total Number of Applications returned because of blocked record._____

_____   _____   _____
Signature of CPL Contact Person   **Date**   **Signature of CPS Recipient**

CHICAGO PUBLIC LIBRARY/ CHICAGO PUBLIC SCHOOLS
RECEIPT FOR LIBRARY CARDS (Copy as Needed)

School_____   CPS representative_____
Phone Number_____   Fax #_____
Library_____   CPL contact person_____
Phone Number_____   Fax #_____

Library Cards Summary

Classroom #	Applications received	Cards Issued	Applications returned-incomplete	Applications returned-blocked record

Total Number of Library Applications dropped off at CPL_____
Total Number of Library Cards Issued from CPL_____
Total Number of Applications returned because incomplete._____
Total Number of Applications returned because of blocked record._____

_____   _____   _____
Signature of CPL Contact Person   **Date**   **Signature of CPS Recipient**

Chicago Public Library/Receipt for Library Cards

CHICAGO PUBLIC LIBRARY
Library Card Campaign

THANK YOU for your library card application.

_____
Child's Name

Our records show that your child:

☐ has materials checked out which have never been returned.
The titles are:

_____

_____

_____

_____   _____

_____

_____

☐ returned materials late and fines are still owed.
Amount due is   _____

☐ did not complete the entire application. Please provide this information:

_____

_____

_____

We are sorry that we cannot issue a library card until these records are cleared.
Please bring this form and the library card application to the branch library noted
below so that we can clear your child's record. We appreciate your interest.

Branch   _____

Address   _____

Phone   _____

Date   _____

Chicago Public Library/Form for Incomplete or Unsuccessful Application

BOOKS ARE ONLY THE BEGINNING
LIBROS SON SOLO EL PRINCIPIO

The Los Angeles Public Library also offers audiotapes, videotapes, computers, author readings, story hours and lots of fun activities for the entire family. It's a whole new place to discover, and it's all right in your neighborhood.

To receive your free card, simply fill out the attached application and return it to any Los Angeles Public Library.

La Biblioteca Pública de Los Angeles también ofrece audiocasetes, vídeos, computadoras, visitas de autores, horas de cuentos y muchas más actividades divertidas para toda la familia. Es un lugar nuevo para descubrir, y todo está en su propio vecindario.

Para recibir su tarjeta gratis, simplemente llene la solicitud incluida y regrésela a cualquier sucursal de la Biblioteca Pública de Los Angeles.

FOR MORE INFORMATION, CALL 1-800-643-LAPL, OR VISIT www.lapl.org.

PARA MÁS INFORMACIÓN LLAME AL 1-800-643-LAPL O VISITE www.lapl.org

SIGN OF INTELLIGENT LIFE IN L.A.
SEÑAL DE VIDA INTELIGENTE EN L.A.

LOS ANGELES PUBLIC LIBRARY

Check it out.

GET YOUR FREE LIBRARY CARD TODAY

OBTENGA SU TARJETA BIBLIOTECARIA GRATIS HOY MISMO

APPLICATION ENCLOSED / SOLICITUD INCLUIDA

22 Harbor Gateway-Harbor City 1555 W. Sepulveda Blvd. (310) 548-7791

23 Hyde Park Branch 6527 Crenshaw Blvd. (323) 750-7241

24 Jefferson Branch – Vassie D. Wright Memorial 2211 W. Jefferson Blvd. (323) 734-8573

25 John C. Fremont Branch 6121 Melrose Ave. (323) 962-3521

26 John Muir Branch 1005 W. 64th St. (323) 789-4800

27 Junípero Serra Branch 4607 S. Main St. (323) 234-1685

28 La Biblioteca del Pueblo de Lincoln Heights Branch 2530 Workman St. (323) 226-1692

29 Little Tokyo Branch 244 S. Alameda St. (213) 612-0525

30 Los Feliz Branch 1874 Hillhurst Ave. (323) 913-4710

31 Loyola Village Branch 7114 W. Manchester Ave. (310) 670-6436

32 Malabar Branch 2801 Wabash Ave. (323) 263-1497

33 Mar Vista Branch 12006 Venice Blvd. (310) 390-3454

34 Mark Twain Branch 9621 S. Figueroa St. (323) 755-4088

35 Memorial Branch 4625 W. Olympic Blvd. (323) 938-2732

36 Mid-Valley Regional Branch & Bookmobile Headquarters 16244 Nordhoff St. (818) 895-3650

37 North Hollywood Regional Branch 5211 Tujunga Ave. (818) 766-7185

38 Northridge Branch 9051 Darby Ave. (818) 886-3640

39 Pacoima Branch 13605 Van Nuys Blvd. (818) 899-5203

40 Palisades Branch 861 Alma Real Dr. (310) 459-2754

41 Palms-Rancho Park Branch 2920 Overland Ave. (310) 838-2157

42 Panorama City Branch 14345 Roscoe Blvd. (818) 894-4071

43 Pío Pico Koreatown Branch 695 S. Serrano Ave. (213) 368-7282

44 Platt Branch 23600 Victory Blvd. (818) 340-9386

45 Porter Ranch Branch 11371 Tampa Ave. (818) 360-5706

46 Robert Louis Stevenson Branch 803 Spence St. (323) 268-4710

47 Robertson Branch 1719 S. Robertson Blvd. (310) 840-2147

48 San Pedro Regional Branch 931 S. Gaffey St. (310) 548-7779

49 Sherman Oaks Branch 14245 Moorpark St. (818) 981-7850

50 Studio City Branch (Closed for construction)

51 Sun Valley Branch 7935 Vineland Ave. (818) 764-7907

52 Sunland-Tujunga Branch 7771 Foothill Blvd. (818) 352-4481

53 Sylmar Branch 13059 Glenoaks Blvd. (818) 367-6102

54 Valley Plaza Branch 12311 Vanowen St. (818) 765-0805

55 Van Nuys Branch 6250 Sylmar Ave. Mall (818) 756-8453

56 Venice – Abbot Kinney Memorial Branch 501 S. Venice Blvd. (310) 821-1769

57 Vermont Square Branch 1201 W. 48th St. (323) 290-7405

58 Vernon Branch – Leon H. Washington Jr. Memorial 4504 S. Central Ave. (323) 234-9106

59 Washington Irving Branch 1803 S. Arlington Ave. (323) 734-6303

60 Alma Reaves Woods – Watts Branch 10205 Compton Ave. (323) 789-2850

61 West Los Angeles Regional Branch 11360 Santa Monica Blvd. (310) 575-8323

62 West Valley Regional Branch 19036 Vanowen St. (818) 345-4393

63 Westchester Branch 8946 Sepulveda Eastway (310) 645-6082

64 Will & Ariel Durant Branch 1403 N. Gardner St. (323) 876-2741

65 Wilmington Branch 1300 N. Avalon Blvd. (310) 834-1082

66 Wilshire Branch 149 N. St. Andrews Pl. (323) 957-4550

67 Woodland Hills Branch 22200 Ventura Blvd. (818) 887-0160

LOS ANGELES PUBLIC LIBRARY

Los Angeles Public Library/Sign of Intelligent Life in LA Brochure/Application

Win one of 25
$100 gift certificates
for your classroom!

APPLICATION RETURN FORM

Just complete this form and the brief evaluation on the back. Attach it to the completed "Wild About Reading" library card applications and mail them in to San José Public Library, using the preaddressed, postage paid envelope provided in your teacher packet.

PLEASE PRINT—

Today's Date:	_____
Teacher:	_____
Room Number:	_____
School Name:	_____
School Address:	_____
City: _____ **Zip:** _____	
School District:	_____

# of students
in class:

_____

# of applications
returned:

_____

FOR RETURNING APPLICATIONS

Receive a free book for your classroom

TEACHER'S NAME: _____

SCHOOL NAME: _____

Thank you for your time!

☞ *Please turn the page and complete*
the brief evaluation form.

FOR RETURNING 100% OF APPLICATIONS

Enter a drawing to win one of 25 $100 gift certificates at your local bookstore.
NOTE: "Check here" and "No thank you" applications count toward 100% return.

TEACHER'S NAME: _____

SCHOOL NAME: _____

Thank you for your time!

San Jose Public Library/ Wild About Reading Application Return Form

 San José Public Library

Parents!

Your first grader is about to begin one of life's great adventures—learning how to read. And your public library is here to help!

Register your child today for a FREE library card and begin a family tradition of regular library visits. On each of the first three visits, your child can claim a free prize—just for using his or her card! What's more important—your child will have free access to a wide variety of books and other materials.

Encourage your child to get *"Wild About Reading!"*

Just complete this simple application and return it to your child's teacher by:

_____ **YES!** I'd like to obtain a free, San José Public Library card for (please print):

CHILD'S NAME: _____
          First Name   Middle Initial   Last Name

CHILD'S MAILING ADDRESS: _____APT/SP #_____

CITY: _____ZIP: _____

CHILD'S BIRTHDATE: _____ / _____ / _____   PHONE: (_____) _____
                    Mo   Dy   Yr   Area Code

MALE ❑   FEMALE ❑

I will assume full responsibility for items checked out on this card.

PARENT/GUARDIAN NAME: _____

PARENT/GUARDIAN SIGNATURE: _____

_____ **CHECK HERE if your child already has an active library card.**
Ask how your child can participate in the "Wild About Reading" incentives program the next time you visit the library.

_____ **NO,** I do not want my child to have a library card.

San Jose Public Library/Wild About Reading Application

Multnomah County Library/Get Carded! Poster

Your passport to the world

Get a Multnomah County Library card now!
October 2 – November 22, 2000

Any Multnomah County kindergarten class with 100% of the students signed up for library cards will be entered in a drawing to win one of five juggling performances by Rhys Thomas.

Classes with 100% of students signed up that do not win a performance will receive a gift certificate from a local bookstore.

Teachers—
Receive a free coffee coupon from Diedrich Coffee People when you send in the library card applications from your class!

Students—
Receive a "Great Library Card Adventure" sticker!

Multnomah County Library/Great Library Card Adventure Poster

Multnomah County Library's
Great Library Card Adventure
Instructions for Teachers

Thank you for being a part of "The Great Library Card Adventure." We want every Multnomah County K-5 student, faculty and staff member to have a Multnomah County Library card.

Get a Free Drink from Starbucks!

You are the key to the success of this project. We know you're busy, so as a reward for participating in the program, we'll send you a free drink coupon from Starbucks when you send in the library card applications from your class. Your students (both those who already have cards and those who get them through the program) will all get "Great Library Card Adventure" stickers.

School Prizes

The school with the highest percentage of students, faculty, and staff signed up for library cards will win:

- a performance of *Green Eggs and Ham & Gertrude McFuzz* by the Northwest Children's Theater at the school, and
- ten new hardcover books for the school media center.

Four runners-up will also receive a performance of *Green Eggs and Ham & Gertrude McFuzz*. Winning schools will be announced by December 15, 1997.

What Do I Do?

_____ 1. Send the enclosed library card applications home with your students who do not already have library cards. The parent/child needs to fill out the front, and *both* need to sign the back of the application before we can make a card.

_____ 2. Collect the completed applications and send them back in the enclosed envelope, attached to the orange tally sheet. To be eligible for prizes, your applications must be postmarked by November 26, 1997.

_____ 3. You'll receive the cards, stickers for your students, and a Starbucks coupon for you within three weeks of the date your applications are postmarked.

A portion of the proceeds from the sale of Pink Martini's *Sympatique* CD, available in all Starbucks stores beginning late October, benefits Multnomah County Library's "Great Library Card Adventure."

- - over - -

Multnomah County Library/Great Library Card Adventure Instructions for Teachers

Multnomah County Library's
Get Carded!
Instructions for Teachers

Thank you for being a part of *Get Carded!* We want every Multnomah County middle and high school student, faculty and staff member to have a Multnomah County Library card.

Special Offers from Local Businesses!

Students, faculty and staff members who already have Multnomah County Library cards or who apply for them during *Get Carded!* will receive a KewlCard with discount offers from the following area businesses:

- Art Media
- B. Dalton Bookseller
- Barnes & Noble
- Bike Gallery
- A Children's Place
- Electric Castle's Wunderland
- Internet Arena

- Noah's Bagels
- Oaks Park
- Powell's Books
- Rocco's Pizza
- Tower Books
- Tower Records
- Waldenbooks

The offers will be good for the month of April 1998. **KewlCards are not available at local libraries; they can only be earned through the School Corps program.**

What Do I Do?

_____ 1. Tally the number of students in your class who already have library cards and give this number to your school's *Get Carded!* coordinator.

_____ 2. Students who do not have library cards should fill out the front and sign the back of the application. *Students under age 13 must also have a parent's signature to get a card.*

_____ 3. Collect the completed applications and return them to your school's *Get Carded!* coordinator. Applications must be postmarked by March 20 to be eligible for KewlCards.

_____ 4. You'll receive the KewlCards by April 1. Library cards will be processed within a few weeks.

Read this first!

Thank you for joining *The Great Library Card Adventure,* the kindergarten library card campaign from the Multnomah County Library School Corps.

Your *Great Library Card Adventure* kit includes:

- Promotional posters;
- Instructions for you (or the person you designate to coordinate the campaign at your school);
- Packets for the kindergarten teachers at your school, including library card applications, a tally sheet (**IMPORTANT!**), and instructions;
- Any additional applications you requested for other students; and
- An envelope you can use to return the applications and tally sheets to us.

If you find anything missing, need extra applications, or have any questions, please contact Jackie Partch at 736-6004 or jacquelp@nethost.multnomah.lib.or.us

Please send me a *Great Library Card Adventure* kit
(Please print)

School Name_____

School Address_____

Your Name _____

Your Phone Number _____

Number of kindergarten classes in your school: _____

Average number of students per kindergarten class: _____

Will other (non-kindergarten) students apply for cards? __Yes __No
If yes, how many additional applications should we send? _____

Multnomah County Library/Great Library Card Adventure Postcard and Kit Information

A Free Card Just for You!

AUSTIN PUBLIC LIBRARY STAR CARD

Your Name Here

1000036282233

You can get a card at school! Return an application to your teacher on time and be a star!

http://www.ci.austin.tx.us/library

Austin Public Library/Star Card Flyer

★STAR CARD★
AUSTIN PUBLIC LIBRARY
YOUTH CARD APPLICATION

Date Entered/Updated

LIBRARY CARD NUMBER (1)

NAME/NOMBRE

FIRST NAME/PRIMER NOMBRE (3)

MI/INICIAL (4)

LAST NAME/APELLIDO (5)

SUFFIX/SUFIJO (6)

C/O

FIRST AND LAST NAME OF PARENT OR GUARDIAN/NOMBRE Y APELLIDO DEL PADRE O APODERADO (7)

ADDRESS/DOMICILIO

STREET/CALLE (9/10) or (18)*

CITY/CIUDAD (11) or (19)*   STATE/ESTADO (12) or (20)*   ZIP/CÓDIGO POSTAL (14) or (21)*

MAILING ADDRESS OF PARENT OR GUARDIAN (if different)/DIRECCIÓN POSTAL DEL PADRE O APODERADO (si es diferente)

STREET OR P.O. BOX/CALLE O CASILLA (9)

CITY/CIUDAD (11)   STATE/ESTADO (12)   ZIP/CÓDIGO POSTAL (14)

PHONE NUMBER/
TELÉFONO (22)

PHONE NUMBER OF PARENT OR GUARDIAN/
TELÉFONO DEL PADRE O APODERADO (7)*

DATE OF BIRTH/FECHA
DE NACIMIENTO (19)

( )   —

AREA CODE/CÓDIGO DEL ÁREA

( )   —

AREA CODE/CÓDIGO DEL ÁREA

M M D D Y Y
(Required/requerido)

IDENTIFICATION - Please provide driver's license or one of the following I.D. numbers.
IDENTIFICACIÓN - Muéstrenos su licencia de manejar o uno de los números de identificación siguientes.

T D L

TEXAS DRIVER'S LICENSE NUMBER (24)

D

TEXAS DEPARTMENT OF PUBLIC SAFETY (23)

U.S. PASSPORT (P) OR RESIDENT ALIEN CARD (R) (23)

STATE   NON-TEXAS OR INTERNATIONAL DRIVER'S LICENSE (24)

I assume responsibility for all materials
checked out on and all charges incurred by
the use of this card. I understand that
Library fees, including card replacement
and non-refundable service charge, are set
by the Austin City Council and are subject
to change. To minimize liability, I will inform
the Library immediately if the card
becomes lost or stolen.

Asumo responsabilidad por todos los
materiales que me han sido prestados y
por todos los cargos contraídos por el uso
de esta tarjeta. Entiendo que los cargos,
incluyendo el costo de reemplazo de la
tarjeta y el costo de servicio sin derecho a
reembolso, son fijados por el Consejo
Municipal de Austin y pueden ser
cambiados. Para minimizar mis deudas,
informaré a la Biblioteca cuando mi tarjeta
se haya perdido o ha sido robada.

X

Signature of Parent or Guardian/Firma del Padre o Apoderado

—   —

SOCIAL SECURITY NUMBER (18)   AND

PHOTO ID: MILITARY, SCHOOL, ETC.*

RE, NR, DO, AC, AF (33)   HOME/REG. BRANCH (31/32)   CLASS (34)   VERIFIER SIGNATURE   DATE

J Y

☐ Mail postmarked in last 30 days
☐ No ID

* Refer to instructions

ALIS 1/00

Austin Public Library/Star Card Application

January 2000

Dear Parent or Guardian:

The Austin Public Library has a goal to provide the opportunity for every young person in the greater Austin area to obtain a youth Star Card free of charge. The Austin Independent School District is working with Austin Public Library to meet this goal.

We encourage you to complete the enclosed form to apply for a Star Card for your student and return it to the school within one week. Information about how to register is included on the back of the form. Please be sure to:

> → fill in your child's full name, including a middle initial;
> → provide one of the identification numbers requested in the ID area at the bottom of the form – a driver's license number is the preferred identification;
> → sign the responsibility statement on the front of the form;
> → go over the responsibility statement on the back of the form with your child and have her/him sign it.

If your child has a Library card that was issued before the new Star Card was implemented November 15, 1999 (it will be pale blue or white), the Library will replace that card with a new Star Card and erase any outstanding fines on the old card when the Star Card is issued.

The new Star Cards will be distributed at school as soon as possible once the Library has received the completed application forms.

If you would prefer to register your child sooner, you may take the application form to any Austin Public Library location. Your child may check out two items, except for CD-ROMs, upon successful application for a Library card at a Library location. If you choose to register at the Library, please return a note to that effect in place of the completed registration form to the school.

If your student already has a Star Card (issued after November 14, 1999), please fill in your student's name and note anywhere on the top of the form that the student already has a Star Card, and return it to the school.

Please contact the Library's Customer Service Office at (512) 499-7402 or your school if you would like any additional information. We look forward to seeing you and your family in the Library to check out materials and participate in a wide range of programs and services. Thank you.

Austin Public Library

Austin Public Library/Star Card "Dear Parent or Guardian" Letter

Walking In Library Doors

Public Library Card
APPLICATION
YES!

I wish to apply for a library card so that I may borrow materials from the library. I agree to follow the library rules and to return all items I borrow in good condition and on time. I will tell the library if my address or phone number changes.

_____
Student's Signature

Name _____ Social Security # _____

Address _____ Apt. # _____

City _____ State _____ Zip _____

Home Phone _____ Date of Birth_____

School _____ Grade_____ Teacher_____

• •
Parent/Guardian Please Read and Complete

I give permission for my child _____ (print name) to borrow materials from the library. I will be responsible for the prompt return of all items borrowed and for any overdue fines, damages, or losses incurred while the materials are on loan to my child.

Parent/Guardian Signature _____

Parent/Guardian Name (printed) _____

Address (if different from child's) _____

City _____ State _____ Zip _____ Day Phone _____

Email Address _____ Evening Phone _____

Driver's License # _____ **(or) Non-Driver's License ID #** _____

Please Circle One: Mother   Father   Legal Guardian (specify) _____

FOR LIBRARY USE ONLY

(BPL) (MUN)

Exp. Date: _____   P Code 1: K   M   P Code 2: _____

P Code 3: _____   P Type: _____   Home Lib. Code: _____

OOC: WAIVED/PAID/VERIFIED   .p # _____

Staff Initials:_____   Bar Code: _____

WB21 WTTO

PEPSI.

Jefferson County JC LC Library Cooperative

A PROJECT TO ENCOURAGE CHILDREN IN JEFFERSON COUNTY TO READ
Sponsored by Pepsi Cola, WTTO Channel 21, and the Jefferson County Library Cooperative

Jefferson County Cooperative/WILD Card Application

APPLICATION

YES!

I wish to apply for a library card so that I may borrow materials from the library. I agree to follow the library rules and to return all items I borrow in good condition and on time. I will tell the library if my address or phone number changes.

_____
Child's Signature

Name _____ Social Security # _____

Street _____ Apt. # _____

City _____ State _____ Zip _____

Home Phone _____ Date of Birth _____

School _____ Grade _____ Teacher _____

∙∙

Parent/Guardian Please Read and Complete

I give permission for my child _____ (print name) to borrow materials from the library. I will be responsible for the prompt return of all items borrowed and for any overdue fines, damages, or losses incurred while the materials are on loan to my child.

Parent/Guardian Signature _____

Parent/Guardian Name (printed) _____

Address (if different from child's) _____

City _____ State _____ Zip _____

Day Phone _____ Evening Phone _____

Driver's License # _____ **(or) Non-Driver's License ID #** _____

Please Circle One: Mother   Father   Legal Guardian (specify) _____

FOR LIBRARY USE ONLY

Exp. Date: _____   P Code 1: K   P Code 2: _____

P Code 3: _____   P Type: 0 1 2 3 4 5 6 7   Home Lib. Code: _____

OOC Verified: __ Y __ N   OOC Pd: __ Y __ N   Bar Code # 21405:_____

.p #: _____   Staff Initials: _____

∙∙∙∙∙∙   BIRMINGHAM PUBLIC LIBRARY—"LICENSED TO READ" PROJECT ∙∙∙∙∙∙

Birmingham Public Library/Licensed to Read Application

Birmingham Public Library/Licensed to Read Poster

**With Your Durham County
Library Card**

**DURHAM COUNTY LIBRARY
DURHAM, NORTH CAROLINA**

GET CONNECTED TO THE WORLD WITH YOUR DURHAM COUNTY LIBRARY CARD!
SIGN UP AND SEE THE WORLD OF POSSIBILITIES...
If you're a new borrower, watch for your invitation to our Open House at the Main Library
on Sunday, October 10. Attend and you could win great prizes provided by Ericsson.
Library Locations can be found on the back of this bookmark

YOU ARE CORDIALLY INVITED TO DURHAM COUNTY LIBRARY'S
TECHNOLOGY OPEN HOUSE
IN RECOGNITION OF YOUR REGISTRATION FOR A NEW LIBRARY CARD DURING
LIBRARY CARD SIGN-UP MONTH. TAKE THIS OPPORTUNITY TO SEE A
DEMONSTRATION OF THE LIBRARY'S MANY NEW TECHNOLOGY-BASED PRODUCTS
AND SERVICES. THE OPEN HOUSE IS BY INVITATION ONLY AND YOU WILL NEED
TO PRESENT THIS POSTCARD UPON ENTRY. THOSE PRESENT WILL BE ENTERED
INTO A DRAWING TO RECEIVE ONE OF THE MANY PRIZES PROVIDED BY ERICSSON.
OUR GRAND PRIZEWINNER WILL RECEIVE A COMPLETE COMPUTER SYSTEM.
OTHER PRIZES INCLUDE CD PLAYERS, CAMERAS, RADIOS AND GIFT CERTIFICATES.

TECHNOLOGY OPEN HOUSE
SUNDAY, OCTOBER 10, 1999
1-2 P.M.
DURHAM COUNTY MAIN LIBRARY
300 N. ROXBORO STREET

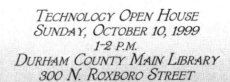

QUESTIONS? CALL 560-0150.

**Durham County Public Library/Technology Open House Invitation and Get Connected
to the World Bookmark**

Sign up today

Explore the universe with a Jefferson County Public Library card

- A million books – magazines – tapes – CDs
- Use of online databases and catalogs at no charge
- Programs and free classes for children and adults

Fill out and mail this application. Or bring it to a Jefferson County Public Library for same-day service. For addresses and phone numbers, see our listing in the U S West Dex Yellow Pages under "Libraries."

fold here

Library use only			
PCODE 1_____	Foundation info_____	Residence_____	Patron Type_____

Name_____
            last name   first name   middle

Mailing address_____

Street address_____

City _____County _____ State <u>CO</u> Zip_____

Home Phone (_____) _____ Work Phone (_____) _____

Birthdate _____ _____ _____
            month   day   year   Email address (optional)_____

I accept responsibility for all materials borrowed and/or all costs incurred. I will report theft or loss of the card or change of address to the library immediately. I understand this card can be revoked at any time. I understand there is a charge for replacement of lost cards. I understand information about my library card may be shared with other Colorado Library Card libraries at their request if my card is used outside the Jefferson County Public Library system.

_____   _____
Patron Signature   (Patrons under 16 must have
                                                          parent/guardian signature here)

_____   _____
Date   **PRINT** name here

                                                          JCPL 430b 6-00

Jefferson County Library/Sign Up Today Application

Volume 1, Issue 1

Summer 2000

Today's Readers are Tomorrow's Leaders
Library Starts Kids' Club

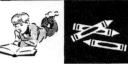

The New Orleans Public Library announces the start of its new **Kids' Club**. The club is for all children who live in New Orleans, and, starting June 5, you can sign up and join the club at any New Orleans Public Library location. Okay, so now you want to know: what is the **Kids' Club** and why you should join?

Kids Club

First of all, **Kids' Club** is for kids only and only kids can join. We at the library wanted to start something special just for you. We wanted to let you know that the library thinks kids are so important that they need their own special library cards, newsletter and fun activities to do at the library.

Plus, we need your help. We would like to know what computer games you like and what kinds of things you like to do—what you like to read about, what you like to draw, and what you want at the library. What magazines would you like? What books would

you like more of? What fun things would you like to do at the library? The **Kids' Club** is your chance to tell us (adults) what YOU WANT!!!!

Hey, let me tell you what the library already has for you. We have lots of books, but, I guess you already knew that. We also have computers, magazines, special programs to go to and, now, a club to join. So, what's stopping you from joining the club? Oh, you want to know what else get?

(club continued on page 3)

LIBRARY FINES FORGIVEN FOR NEW KIDS CLUB MEMBERS

Amnesty is defined in *Random House Webster's Dictionary* as "a general pardon." Another way to say this is that amnesty means "to forgive

something."

What that means is if you owe any fines— money that is paid to the library when books are brought back later than the day when they are supposed to be returned—

the library will forgive your fines up to the amount of $10. This will be done when you sign up as a **Kids' Club** member. So, act now, this is a one time offer good until August 5, 2000.

This newsletter printed with funds from Carnegie Corporation of New York.

Kids' Club Application

- ◆ If you already have a card, fill out this application.
- ◆ If you don't have a card yet, you will need to go to the nearest library with one of your parents to fill out a library card application.

1. Name_____School Name_____

2. Date of Birth_____ Library Card #_____

3. What do you like to read about?_____

4. What do you like to do on a computer?_____

5. What do you like to draw _____
       Remember, we need art work for our "Kids' Page" and our newsletter.

6. What do you like to write? Stories?_____   Poems?_____

What subjects do you like to write about?
_____
_____

New Orleans Public Library/Kids Club Application

Mayor and Mrs. Rimsza and the Phoenix Public Library
proudly present

Congratulations!

Here is your very own GOAL library card!

Phoenix Public Library/Congratulations Brochure (outside)

Here is your GOAL card.

Bookbreath says,

" Take good care of your card. Read every day."

Prizes for visiting the Phoenix Public Library!

First visit   = Necklace card holder
Second visit = Bookbag
Third visit   = Pencil

EARN ALL THREE PRIZES!

Phoenix Public Library/Congratulations Brochure (inside)

Phoenix Public Library/Project GOAL Poster

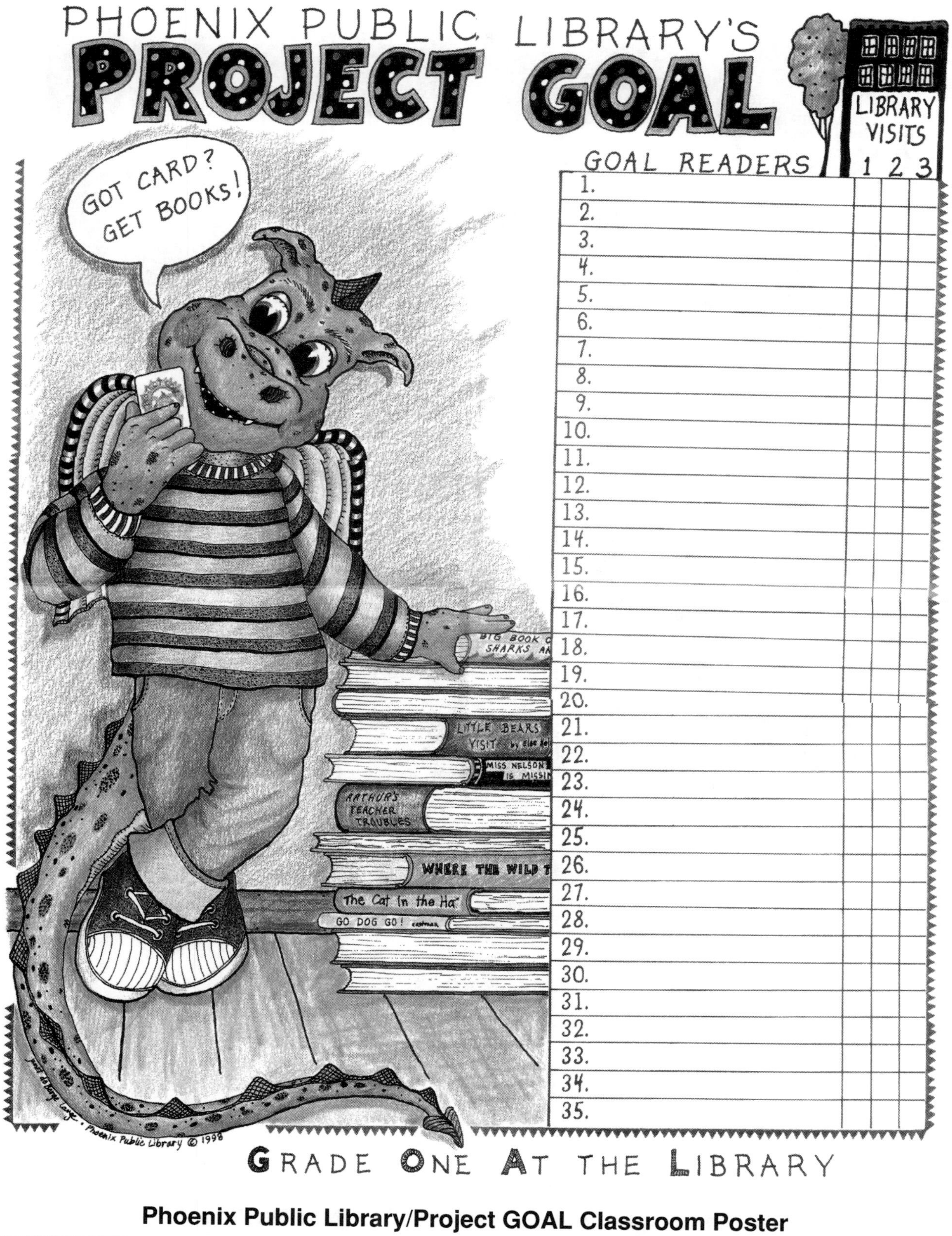

Phoenix Public Library/Project GOAL Classroom Poster

Pikes Peak Library District/Just Say "Yes" to the KNOWcard Brochure

 What?

You can have your very own library card —

KNOW CARD

and it's free!

You can check out ...

videos, books, CDs
CD-ROMs, tapes,
magazines, !

PIKES PEAK LIBRARY DISTRICT

 CARD

It's your first charge card — and the most important one you'll ever use.

With your free **KNOW CARD** from the Pikes Peak Library District, you can find out just about anything you'll ever need to know.

Be sure you check with your parents to see what types of things they want you to check out with your **KNOW CARD** .

Here's how to get
KNOW CARD

Fill out the application in this brochure and take it to:

✓ your school librarian or

✓ any Pikes Peak Library District branch.

Happy reading!

Pikes Peak Library District/KNOW What Brochure

KNOW THE POWER...
KNOW THE POSSIBILITIES...
WITH THE

...IT'S FREE!

IT'S YOURS!
IT'S BETTER THAN A CHARGE CARD!

VIDEOS BOOKS MAGAZINES CDS TAPES CD-ROMS NEWSPAPERS INTERNET ENTERTAINMENT JOBS EDUCATION AND LOTS MORE!

PIKES PEAK LIBRARY DISTRICT

A LIBRARY CARD — THE KNOW CARD

With your free library card from the Pikes Peak Library District, you can find out just about anything you'll ever need to know. You can use your " **KNOW** CARD" to check out anything from the library's circulating collection and get access to subscription databases on the library's WEBsite.

HERE'S HOW TO GET THE KNOW CARD

Fill out the application in this brochure and take it to:

• your school librarian or

• any Pikes Peak Library District branch.

Pikes Peak Library District/KNOW the Power Brochure

THE KNOW CARD

Yes! I want to help raise children's reading scores by providing all of my students with a library card, the Pikes Peak Library District's KNOW CARD. I would also like to take advantage of the following library services:

❑ a tour of the library for my class
- grade _____
- library branch _____

❑ a demonstration of reference databases on the library's WEBsite that are of interest to educators

❑ a demonstration of reference databases on the library's WEBsite that are of interest to my students
- grade _____

❑ book talks
- grade _____

❑ e-mail receipt of library press releases
- e-mail address

_____

❑ e-mail receipt of reading lists, etc.
- e-mail address

_____

❑ in-school storytime

Name _____

School _____

School Address _____

Telephone # _____

Please return this to your library liaison with students' library card applications. You will be contacted to set up dates and times. Thank you!

PL PIKES PEAK LIBRARY DISTRICT

P.O. Box 1579 · Colorado Springs, CO 80901-1579 · (719) 531-6333 · http://library.ppld.org

Pikes Peak Library District/KNOWcard Teacher Letter

KNOW CARD INFORMATION

School Name: _____
(complete)

Elementary Middle School Junior High
Middle School Charter Private Alternative Other

Number students enrolled: _____

PPLD KNOW Card Committee Representative: _____

Address: _____ City: _____ Zip Code: _____ Phone #: _____

E-mail: _____ School Contact's Name: _____

Date of first contact: _____

Follow-Up:
Date: _____
Time: _____

School Visit Data

Visit Date: _____

Evening Open House #
Pre-registration Event
Student Assembly
Classroom Visit
Kindergarten Visit
New Student Enrollee Visit

Narrative of visit:

OFFICE USE ONLY

# of new cards issued: _____
# of replacement cards issues: _____
# of total cards issued: _____
Data entered by: _____
Branch Names: _____
Staff Initials: _____ Date: _____

Please return this form to Tina Webster at East Circulation

Pikes Peak Library District/KNOWcard Tally Sheet

PIKES PEAK LIBRARY DISTRICT

Pikes Peak Library District
"Fast & Easy"
KNOWcard Registration Process for Schools

The Pikes Peak Library District is providing every student in twelve school districts a new or replacement library card -- the KNOWcard. Last year the library KNOWcard Team visited 48 schools and registered 100 percent of the students in each school.

Working with the media specialist or CIT and a streamlined process, the KNOWcard Team simultaneously registers students ten classes at a time. *We can provide library cards to a school of 700 students in about two hours.*

The library will customize your KNOWcard visit, including:
✓ Present the benefits of the *KNOWcard* at a faculty meeting.
✓ Attend a planning meeting with the school media specialist or CIT.
✓ Assist to select a time of day at which most students are seated in class.
✓ Provide *Parent Notification* flyers for students (attached).
✓ Prepare (in bundles of 30) age-appropriate library card application and bar-coded library cards for # of classes in the school, and Spanish applications for ESL students.
✓ Assign library staff to classrooms based on color-coded school floor plan (by grade, floor, section of the building or whatever works best)
✓ Register ten classes at a time – about 15 minutes per class.
✓ Activate the library cards within three days.
✓ Customize database training for school faculty, and provide book lists, book talks and other support to classroom teachers.

How your principal or media specialist can facilitate the process:
✓ Select the best day for the KNOWcard Team visit.
✓ Notify classroom teachers of the time and day of the visit.
✓ Distribute Parent Notification flyers to teachers to distribute to students.
✓ Include information about the visit in the school newsletter.
✓ Determine the total number of classrooms to visit.
✓ "Color code" school floor plans and make ten copies for KNOWcard Team. (Example attached)
✓ (K- 4 ONLY: Affix name and address labels to library card applications by class, or provide labels by class and library staff can affix in advance.)
✓ Allow 15 minutes per class to register every student with a new or replacement library card.

To schedule a KNOWcard visit to your school, please contact:
Nancy Milvid, KNOWcard Campaign Coordinator
531-6333 x 1251 or nmilvid@mail.ppld.org

❏ PENROSE PUBLIC LIBRARY
20 N. Cascade Ave. 80903

❏ EAST LIBRARY AND INFORMATION CENTER
5550 N. Union Blvd. 80918

MAILING ADDRESS: P.O. BOX 1579 • COLORADO SPRINGS, CO 80901-1579 • (719) 531-6333 • TELEFAX (719) 528-5259 • http://library.ppld.org
■ Cheyenne Mountain ■ Fountain ■ Monument Hill ■ Old Colorado City ■ Palmer Lake ■ Rockimmon ■ Ruth Holley ■ Sand Creek ■ Ute Pass

Pikes Peak Library District/KNOWcard Registration Process for Schools Flyer

Dear Parents,

Kids who read succeed!

The Pikes Peak Library District's "**KNOW**card Team" is coming to your child's school next week to issue free library cards to students.

A library card number gives your child access to selected and purchased computer databases for:
- help with homework,
- "Ask a Librarian" for e-mail help answering questions and
- facts, pictures and information for reports.

Even if someone in your family already has a card, it is important for each student to have his or her own **KNOW**card. Students will receive their new or free replacement card at school next week. Cards will be processed and activated in about five working days.

We look forward to being a partner in your child's lifelong learning and love for books. Visit your nearest library soon! Thank you.

Sincerely,

Nancy Milvid, **KNOW**card Campaign Coordinator
Pikes Peak Library District
531-6333, x1251   nmilvid@mail.ppld.org

Pikes Peak Library District/KNOWcard Letter to Parents

KNOW THE POWER . . .

Pikes Peak Library District
KNOWcard

What is the KNOWcard campaign?

The Pikes Peak Library District wants everyone to KNOW the power of reading. Our goal is for every school-aged child in the library district to have a library card.

What is a KNOWcard?

The KNOWcard is the new name for a plastic card from the Pikes Peak Library District (PPLD).

Who can get a KNOWcard?

The KNOWcard is available, free, to all children and adults living within the Pikes Peak Library District — most of El Paso County — including School Districts # 1, 2, 8, 11,12, 20, 22, 23, 28, 38, 49, 54, and 60.

Where can I use the KNOWcard?

You can use your KNOWcard at any of the district's 11 library facilities, two bookmobiles or on the Internet Branch. And, because PPLD is part of the Colorado Library Card program, you can use it at every participating library in the state.

What are the benefits of a KNOWcard?

Research shows that "kids who read succeed." Your KNOWcard gives you a jumpstart on success – success in school and in **everything** you do! You also gain the power that comes from reading and access to information.

What is unique about the KNOWcard?

Besides having access to over *a million* books, videos, CDs, tapes, and magazines, you can get homework help on the library's Internet Branch with your KNOWcard. Your library card number gives you special access to:

- "Ask a Librarian" for e-mail help answering quick, factual questions,
- full-text magazine articles under "magazines,"
- pictures and graphics like state flags and maps on SIRS DISCOVERER,
- an Animal Encyclopedia in SEARCHASARUS,
- ENCYCLOPEDIA AMERICAN or GROLIER'S ENCYCLOPEDIA,
- kids' encyclopedias under SEARCHASARUS and SIRS DISCOVERER,
- fast facts, full-text articles, book lists and specific web resources for thousands of people from Martin Luther King to Ricky Martin, under BIOGRAPHY RESOURCE CENTER,
- facts about authors and book lists under LITERATURE RESOURCE CENTER,
- web sites for common school assignments under HOMEWORK HELPERS,
- an almanac, dictionary and thesaurus for students under SIRS DISCOVERER,
- book suggestions that kids your age like under NOVELIST and UNDER 18 – YA ZONE,
- reserving books online.

Where can I get more information?

Contact your local branch library or the main libraries of the Pikes Peak Library District – Penrose Public Library or the East Library and Information Center – at 531-6333.

Check out our WEBsite at http://library.ppld.org

PIKES PEAK LIBRARY DISTRICT

Pikes Peak Library District/KNOWcard Fact Sheet

KNOW WHAT?

Students can raise reading scores by using the public library.

★ **Reading scores are higher in communities with public libraries that have high circulation of children's materials.**

In Colorado school districts scoring in the highest third on the 1997 CSAP reading test, circulation of children's materials per capita by public libraries was 50% higher than in school districts scoring in the lowest third.

Similarly, in states scoring in the highest third on the 1994 NAEP reading test, circulation of children's materials per capita by public libraries was more than a third higher than in states scoring in the lowest third. [1]

★ **Reading scores are higher for children who attend schools with well-managed library media programs that cooperate with local public libraries.**

In 1997, 4th grade students in schools with well-planned library media programs and well-documented collection development policies, and whose relationships with their public library included book talks and summer reading programs, averaged reading scores up to 15 points higher in the Colorado Student Assessment Program than those without such LM programs. [2]

★ **Reading scores are higher for children who spend time reading outside of school.**

"Education researchers Anne Cunningham and Keith Stanovich found that kids who read at the 98th percentile read an average of 65 minutes a day outside of school, while students at the 50th percentile — the very definition of average readers — read only about four-and-a-half minutes a day. For children at the 20th percentile, the time spent reading outside of school amounted to zero." [3]

KNOW HOW?

Help students get their own free library card — the KNOW card!

Join the Pikes Peak Library District's KNOW card campaign, part of a larger vision of building assets for youth and a literate, informed community.

With a KNOW card. . .

★ **Check out books, videos, CDs, magazines, CD-ROMs, audiocassettes**

★ **Access E-Reference databases on your home or public library PC at http://library.ppld.org**

Encyclopedia Americana
Contemporary Authors
Health Source Plus
Colorado Newspaper Bundle
Searchasaurus
Community Connections
All-in-one Magazine Search and lots more

★ **Plus, visit the KidsWeb and the YA Zone pages on the library's WEBsite for information specific to kids' needs and interests.**

★ **Discover incentives to keep students reading through the Summer Reading Programs.**

[1] Source: *Fast Facts: Recent Statistics from The Library Research Service.* 10/22/98

[2] Source: *Fast Facts: Recent Statistics from The Library Research Service.* 10/7/98

[3] Mettner, Jeanne, *"Just Read It.* (Importance of starting early reading habit in children)" MPLS-St. Paul Magazine (May 1999) v.27 i5:p.116(1)

PIKES PEAK LIBRARY DISTRICT

Pikes Peak Library District/Inform, Empower, Inspire Flyer

HAPPY BIRTHDAY TO YOU,
HAPPY BIRTHDAY TO YOU,
HAPPY BIRTHDAY DEAR

_____

Richmond Memorial Library would like to wish you a very special day on _____ . As a reward for registering for a library card, bring this letter to the *Children's Room*, where you may select a book from the collection where a bookplate will be placed in the front of it bearing your name. Everyone who takes that book out will know you are a special library user!

Remember, reading is the best present you can give yourself!!

HAPPY BIRTHDAY,
RICHMOND LIBRARY STAFF

Richmond Public Library/Happy Birthday Flyer

FOUNTAINDALE PUBLIC LIBRARY DISTRICT

300 West Briarcliff Road **Bolingbrook, IL 60440** **(630) 759-2102 Fax 759-9519** **Children's Services, Ext. 16**	**201 Normantown Road** **Romeoville, IL 60446** **(815) 886-2030 Fax 886-0686** **Children's Services, Ext. 28**

September, 2000

Dear Parents and Guardians:

KIDS WHO READ SUCCEED

One of the most important school supply items for your child is a library card. But did you know that a library card is FREE?

If your child does not already have a library card, an application is below. Fill it in, return it to the library, and receive a card for your child. It's just that easy.

All students in grades K-5 with a library card (including new cardholders) are invited to fill out the "Battle of the Cards" entry form below. Return the form to Children's Services at Fountaindale Library in Bolingbrook or Romeoville. Those children returning their own forms will receive a special prize from Children's Services.

Returned forms will enter your school in the 2nd annual "Battle of the CARDS!" The winning schools will receive paperback book collections for their Library Media Centers. Children living outside the Fountaindale Public Library District may bring in their library card from the issuing library to receive a Fountaindale Library card barcode. This will permit your child to check out materials and participate in the "Battle".

The winning schools in Bolingbrook and Romeoville will be those with the highest percentage of entry forms returned for NEW and EXISTING LIBRARY CARDS. All entries must be returned by October 31. If you have any questions, please contact Carol Feldberg in Bolingbrook (630-759-2102, Ext. 16) or Racheal Perek in Romeoville (815-886-2030, Ext. 28).

Happy Reading!

Carol Feldberg BB and Racheal Perek RV
Children's Services

"BATTLE OF THE CARDS!"
Entry Form for New and Existing Card Holders

Name_____
Library Card Number_____
School Name_____

Please fill out and return to Children's Services by October 31st. Thank You.
Entry forms not completely filled out will be disqualified.

Application for 1st Time Library Card Holders

I apply for the right to use the library and will abide by the Library's rules. I will pay fines or damages charged to me and I will give prompt notice of change of address or lost card.

Last Name_____
First Name_____
Address_____Zip_____
Subdivision_____Grade of Child_____
Phone_____
Parent Signature_____

Fountaindale Public Library/Battle of the Cards Flyer

PROCLAMATION

WHEREAS, Missoula Public Library has always offered a wealth of books, magazines and reference resources; today we also offer videotapes, audiotapes, computers, Internet access for every age, children's programs and other resources that can give every child a head start on learning.

WHEREAS, September is Library Card Sign-up Month; a time when the American Library Association and Missoula Public Library remind you to make sure you and your family have the most important card of all, one available free to everyone in Montana.

NOW, THEREFORE, I, Mike Kadas, Mayor of the City of Missoula, in the State of Montana, do hereby proclaim September, 2000 as

Library Card Sign-up Month

in Missoula, Montana.

IN WITNESS WHEREOF, I have hereunto set my hand and caused the great seal of the City of Missoula, in the State of Montana, to be affixed at Missoula, Montana, this 11th day of August, in the year of our Lord, two thousand.

ML Kadas

Mike Kadas
Mayor

Missoula Public Library/Proclamation

OVERDUE FINES GOT YOU DOWN?? presenting....

"FOOD FOR FIDO"
(brought to you by Missoula Public Library and The Humane Society Animal Shelter)

100% OFF FINES!

Tel: 406-721-2665

WHEN?
SEPTEMBER 12TH-14TH
(3 DAYS ONLY)

WHERE?
MISSOULA PUBLIC LIBRARY CIRCULATION DESK

WHAT?
BRING IN ANY PET FOOD OR SUPPLY ITEM TO HAVE YOUR OVERDUE FINES WAIVED

NO LIVE DONATIONS ACCEPTED!!!!

Missoula Public Library/Food for Fido Flyer

Winners Announced!

During the month of September, the Missoula Public Library participated in a national effort to encourage people to get a library card. To our delight, the library now has over 600 new borrowers as a result. Participants also entered drawings and contests.

Nearly 60 "library lovers" entered the "Why I Love My Library Card" contest. They were asked to explain "what it is that brings you to Missoula Public Library — what do you love about the library?" The results were outstanding and it was very difficult to select winners in the adult and children's categories. The winning writers won donated gift certificates.

First prize in the adult category went to **Ruth Harris**. Here is her alliterative essay.

Lustrous and legible, library cards let lads and lassies loose to linger in lavish lines of literature. Lending libraries launch literacy in larithmics, law, limnology, legerdemain, and linguistics. Lords and ladies luxuriate in locating Lisbon, LaMancha, London, and Luxembourg. Little ones listen to lore about leprechauns, lobsters, and lagomorphs. Librettists look in large lexicons. Lawyers learn of legislation. <u>Little Women</u>, <u>Little Men</u>, <u>Little Lord Fauntleroy</u>, and <u>The Little Prince</u> lure loyal literati to light a lamp and lift their leaves. Liverpudlians like Lofting, Lamb, and Lawrence. Lethargy languishes when literature lends light. Librarys' largess lubricates love of learning.

In the 0-13 category, **Caleb Harris** penned this poem to win:

I love the library
I think it so fine
If it were for sale
It'd prob'ly be mine

That little grey card
That I stick in a nook
I bring it on over
When I want a book

From classics to sci-fi
You have everything
If I need some service
I just have to ring

I like all your books
And your videos too
If anyone has it
It's probably you

When it's time to leave
I look back with a sigh
But I know that next week
I'll be sure to drop by.

Thanks to all who entered the contests, and to the Friends of Missoula Public Library and area businesses who generously provided the prizes and certificates.

Missoula Public Library/Winning Contest Entries

Traci Welch Moritz
Youth Services Coordinator

Putnam County District Library
525 N. Thomas St
Ottawa, OH 45875
419-523-3747

April 17, 2001

Dear Parents of a first grader,

Your child has brought home information on how to get his/her very own library card. This is an excellent opportunity to encourage a love of reading. Studies have shown over and over that those who read succeed. How exciting for children to get to come to the library, pick out a book and take it home! Plus, it is a great way to teach responsibility and how to care for library materials. I love this time when kids are just learning to read and their eyes light up when they recognize a new word!

Your child's teacher has made it possible for your first grader to visit the library on Monday, May 14th for a tour and a program. If you fill out the form <u>completely</u> and return it to the teacher no later than Friday, April 27th your child will receive their library card on the day of the tour and he/she will be able to check out 1 book. (Please let the teacher know if you do not want your child to select a book). If your child already has a library card, please send it to school the 14th. Should there be fines or if you need to replace a lost card, please do so before the visit. Parents are responsible for seeing that the book your child checks out this day is returned to the library.

All children's books circulate for 4 weeks now (with no renewals) and children's magazines go out for 1 week. Kids aren't eligible to check out videos.

It is extremely important that you fill out the green card completely with the child's information and the parents' signature. All of the information requested on the white sheet must be completed with the child's information on the top and the adult's information on the bottom. If you have any questions at all, please call the library at 523-3747.
This card is for use at the Main Library in Ottawa and any of the branches in Continental, Columbus Grove, Kalida, Fort Jennings, Leipsic, Pandora, or Ottoville.

Sincerely,

Traci Welch Moritz
Youth Services Coordinator

Putnam County Library/Dear Parent Letter

Celebrate National Library Card Sign-up Month

with

Arthur at the Library!

Monday, September 18
4:00-5:30 & 7:00-8:30 P.M.
Centerville Library

- *Meet Arthur in person!*
- *Take a picture with Arthur!*
- *Sign up for a library card!*
- *Do fun activities!*
- *Listen to stories!*

Anyone needing special accommodations to attend should contact the library in advance.

Washington-Centerville Public Library

Centerville Library	**Woodbourne Library**
111 W. Spring Valley Road	6060 Far Hills Avenue
Centerville, Ohio 45458	Centerville, Ohio 45459
(937) 433-8091	(937) 435-3700

www.wcpl.lib.oh.us

Washington-Centerville Public Library/Program Flyer

free !
library card

McDonald's®
Supports
South Carolina's
Ticket To Read

Have a parent or guardian come with you and

bring something with your address on it.

It's that easy.

"We need to teach our children that the most valuable possession a kid can have is not a new pair of Nikes® or a Game Boy™...it's a library card."

–Governor Jim Hodges
1999 State of the State Address

smile™

TICKET TO read

Hey kids! Did you know that with a free library card you can....**Borrow cool books** for fun and school work! **Use computers** and **the Internet!** Borrow **videos, cassettes and CDs!** Read **the latest magazines! Find answers** to your questions! **Research** what you want to be when you grow up! Be a part of **story hours, arts and crafts,** and **other programs!** Join a **summer reading program!** All of it can be yours when you get a **free library card** today at your public library...your **ticket to read!**

PRINTED ON RECYCLED PAPER 10% Post Consumer Content 90% Pre-consumer Content   © 2001 McDonald's Corporation   VOX 130431-3

South Carolina State Library/McDonald's Tray Mat

South Carolina State Library/Ticket to Read Poster

TICKET TO READ LIBRARY CARD CAMPAIGN
REPORT FORM

School: _____

Address: _____

Media Specialist: _____

A. _____ Total Number of students who had public library cards before this library card campaign began (students who signed on left side of poster)

B. _____ Total number of students with new library cards (students who signed on right side of poster)

C. _____ Total number with library cards at the end of the campaign (A + B)

D. _____ Total number of students in the school:

How effective was this library card promotion in your school?

What suggestions do you have for future library card promotions?

Please evaluate the materials:

	Poor	Adequate	Good	Excellent
Poster				
Brochure				
Handbook				

Other comments:

Please return to: Jane G. Connor   You may also e-mail your
                   Youth Services Consultant   statistics and comments to
                   South Carolina State Library Janec@leo.scsl.state.sc.us
                   P.O. Box 11469
                   Columbia, SC 29211 Fax: 803-734-8676
http://www.state.sc.us/scsl/ticket-to-read.html

South Carolina State Library/Ticket to Read Report Form

Why Children Should Have A Public Library Card

- Children can get great books at the public library for enjoyment, to get answers to questions, to practice reading skills, and to find information for assignments.

- The library also has magazines, videotapes, cassette tapes and CD's of music, stories, and books.

- The Internet and DISCUS—South Carolina's Virtual Library—are available in every public library and public school. A library card also entitles residents access to many of the DISCUS resources from their home Internet accounts. DISCUS includes databases for elementary and middle school students.

- Most public libraries have weekend and evening hours.

LIBRARY CARDS ARE FREE AT PUBLIC LIBRARIES IN THE COUNTY WHERE YOU LIVE. If books and other materials are returned or renewed by the due date, it will not cost anything to borrow from the public library.

Together the public library and school library media center provide the resources students need for school success and personal development.

Sponsored by the South Carolina State Library, South Carolina Association of School Librarians and your public library.

South Carolina State Library/Ticket to Read Information Sheet

RESOURCES

BOOKS AND JOURNALS

"ALA card campaign gets underway." *School Library Journal* 34(August 1988): 21–22.

"Arthur speaks up for library cards." *American Libraries* 31 (September 2000): 8–9.

"Baltimore County Public Library's 'WOW' card." *The Unabashed Librarian* 89 (1993): 3–7.

Behler, Patt.–"For every child in Missouri: A library card." *Show-Me Libraries* 39 (December 1987): 3.

"Bennett opens card campaign: W. Va. sets pace for states." *American Libraries* 18 (November 1987): 815–816.

Bly, Linda. "The gateway card: An experiment in cooperation." *Arkansas Libraries* 55 (October 1998): 19–21.

"Boston PL registers 32,000 new patrons: Electronic card system draws in new registrants." *Library Journal* 115 (March 15, 1990): 20.

Bradburn, Frances Bryant. "The policeman within: Library access issues for children and young adults." *North Carolina Libraries* 51 (Summer 1993): 69–71.

Bradbury, Dan. "Kansas City Public offers statewide library card and free catalog access." *Show-Me Libraries* 42 (Fall 1990): 6–7.

Budler, Jo. "A tale of two visions . . . or achieving goals through amnesia: Statewide library card system in Nebraska." *Nebraska Library Association Quarterly* 28 (Summer 1997): 15–16.

"Card campaigns: Publicity and programs." *School Library Journal* 34 (August 1988): 94.

Caywood, Carolyn A. "Parents, kids, librarians: Can this relationship be saved?" *American Libraries* 30 (June/July 1999): 74.

Chelton, Mary K. "Issues in youth access to library services." *School Library Media Quarterly* 14 (Fall 1985): 21–25.

Clark, Marilyn L. "Toledo and Dayton go for 'library cards for all.'" *Ohio Libraries* 2 (March/April 1989): 6–7.

"The Colorado library card program." *Colorado Libraries* 18 (June 1992): 12.

Colvin, Gloria. "Statewide reciprocal borrowing in Florida." *Florida Libraries* 43 (Spring 2000): 7.

"Competition set for sign-up month." *School Library Journal* 35 (July 1989): 13.

Cummins, Julie. "Write of passage: Registering for a library card." *School Library Journal* 31 (November 1984): 80.

DiMattia, Susan Smith. "Broward County Library debuts BIG card." *Library Journal* 121 (March 15, 1996): 17.

Dixon, Judith. "Are we childproofing our public libraries? Identifying the barriers that limit library use by children." *Public Libraries* 35 (January/February 1996): 50.

Edwards, Leroy V. "Go for the card: A school and public library partnership put to the test." *Ohio Media Spectrum* 42 (Winter 1990): 34–36.

Gerhardt, Lillian Noreen. "Restricted borrowing." *School Library Journal* 40 (May 1994): 4.

Glick, Andrea. "Fight over kids' access rages in Oklahoma City." *School Library Journal* 43 (May 1997): 12.

Goldberg, Beverly. "California laws force trustees to revisit access for minors." *American Libraries* 31 (February 2000): 12.

Gordon, Ruth I. "I helped children lie." *School Library Journal* 41 (February 1995): 42.

"Grade One at the Library: To ensure that each Phoenix first-grader has a library card and, more importantly, begins using it, the city has introduced Grade One at the Library (GOAL)." *Nation's Cities Weekly* (January 11, 1999): 11.

Hildebrand, Janet. "Is privacy reserved for adults? Children's rights at the public library." *School Library Journal* 37 (January 1991): 21–25.

Indiana State Library. "Public library access card questions and answers for public library boards and library staff." *The Unabashed Librarian* 86 (1993): 24–32.

"Key ring library card at Cedar Rapids Public Library." *American Libraries* 23 (October 1992): 730.

Kniffel, Leonard. "Children's access: Protection or preparation?" *American Libraries* 30 (November 1999): 59–62.

Kniffel, Leonard. "Virginia Beach mom wants her kid's borrowing restricted." *American Libraries* 25 (January 1994): 9.

"LA Public launches child card campaign." *School Library Journal* 37 (April 1991): 16.

Lamb, Kurt H. "Project SMILE: A reading and library card promotion for children." *Show-Me Libraries* 38 (September 1987): 8–11.

Landgraf, Mary N. "Library cards for the homeless." *American Libraries* 22 (November 1991): 946–947+.

"Library card campaign continues with new month, new focus, corporate support." *Show-Me Libraries* 39 (Summer 1988): 21–22.

"Library card kickoff honors 100-percenters." *American Libraries* 18 (December 1987): 884.

Lilly, Dorothy. "School and public libraries go online." *Book Report* 11 (September/October 1992): 24–25.

McCarthy, Mary. "The day I got my first library card." *The Unabashed Librarian* 85 (1992): 25.

McCormick, Edith. "Restraints on children's access create controversy at Oak Lawn Public Library." *American Libraries* 21 (July/August 1990): 628.

Meyer, Randy. "Furor over R-rated videos sparks library legislation." *School Library Journal* 42 (April 1996): 11.

"Minnesota library wins sign-up contest." *School Library Journal* 35 (December 1989): 14.

"National library card campaign kicked off on D.C. mall." *School Library Journal* 34 (December 1987): 13.

"The NebrasKard statewide library card: Your information connection across Nebraska." *Nebraska Library Association Quarterly* 29 (Spring 1998): 30–31.

Needham, George M. "Kids + videos = a library dilemma: Open video circulation policy challenged at Akron-Summit County Public Library." *Ohio Libraries* 3 (January/February 1990): 4–5.

Nyfeler, Suzan. "Kids and confidentiality: Balancing privacy with parents' rights." *Texas Libraries* 54 (Fall 1993): 103.

Oder, Norman. "LJ's third annual 1999 politician of the year: Lee Brown." *Library Journal* 124 (September 15, 1999): 22–25.

Olson, Renée. "Brooklyn PL offers children's limited access card." *School Library Journal* 42 (July 1996): 8–9.

"Orange County PL goes for the gold." *Library Journal* 120 (August 1995): 16.

"Prince George's wins public relations award for library card campaign." *Wilson Library Bulletin* 62 (January 1988): 11.

Ptacek, William. "Question: Should there be a state wide library card issued for all citizens in the state of Washington?" *Alki* 9 (December 1993): 9.

"Read Out and library cards successful in West Virginia." *Library Journal* 112 (December 1987): 35.

"Restricted card defeated in Oak Lawn." *School Library Journal* 36 (August 1990): 16.

Rogers, Michael. "AL issues virtual library cards." *Library Journal* 125 (April 15, 2000): 27.

Rollock, Barbara T. "Children have rights: Open access to library resources." *The Bookmark* (Albany, N.Y.) 47 (Winter 1989): 104–105.

Sadowski, Michael J. "New St. Louis policy raises questions of parental control." *School Library Journal* 40 (May 1994): 10–11.

Shapiro, Leila. "Handling applications and permission slips: Simplified registration for library cards." *The Unabashed Librarian* 111 (1999): 8.

Sibley, Celestine. "New library card: A ticket to borrow wealth of wonders." *The Unabashed Librarian* 77 (1990): 15–16.

Smith, Ted. "Free library service for all: A discussion of NebrasKard; or, Don't hate me because I'm dutiful!" *Nebraska Library Association Quarterly* 31 (Spring 2000): 20–21.

Taylor, Deborah D. "Youth access: The most basic value." *School Library Journal* 35 (October 1989): 37–38.

Thorson, Kristine Hoy. "Age discrimination and library cards." *School Library Journal* 35 (May 1988): 53.

"Thousands receive cards in national sign-up campaign." *School Library Journal* 35 (October 1988): 14.

Ticket to read: Library card campaign for elementary schools in South Carolina. Columbia: South Carolina State Library: South Carolina Association of School Librarians, 2000.

Wallace, Linda. "Library card campaign launched in Year of the Reader." In *The ALA yearbook of library and information services,* vol. 13, 106–107. Chicago: American Library Association, 1988.

"Whose card is it anyway?" *American Libraries* 22 (June 1991): 489.

Wigg, Ristiina, "Registering new children at the library: The New York State 'best gift' campaign." *The Bookmark* (Albany, N.Y.) 46 (Spring 1988): 188.

Zhang Xiao Yuan. "An initial study on the relationship between the rate of utilization of borrowers' cards and the time of card-holders holding cards in public libraries." *Public Library Quarterly* 14, no. 1 (1994): 39–52.

NEWSPAPER ARTICLES

Acevedo, Carlos. "Libraries recruiting younger readers: Drive urges parents to get kids signed up for cards." *Spokane (Wash.) Spokesman-Review,* 28 September 2000, N8.

Anderson, Lynn. "Essex library scores a first as tots become cardholders. Preschoolers: In an effort to get children interested in reading at a young age, a Baltimore County library branch has launched 'My First, Library Card.'" *Baltimore Sun,* 21 November 1999, 2B.

Boone, Dana. "Library cards enable youths to ride buses." *Des Moines Register,* 28 June 2000, 1.

Bowie, Liz. "Library offers pupils cards: Baltimore school officials hope giving out public library cards will encourage youngsters to read." *Baltimore Sun,* 29 November 1998, 2B.

Burbach, Chris. "Get library card at mall." *Omaha World-Herald,* 17 April 1999, 13.

"Carded: Every child should have library's new Power Card." *Houston Chronicle,* 2 August 1998, sec. C, col. 1, p. 2.

Cohen, Mark Francis. "Kids' library cards rated 'R,' for restricted." *New York Times,* 7 April 1996, sec. CY, col. 1, p. 9.

Deck, Carole. "Library cards kick off reading reveries: Libraries, schools team up to encourage children's 'ticket to adventure.'" *Intelligencer Journal,* 6 September 2000, B-1.

Gray, Chris. "Water bills will include library cards." *New Orleans Times-Picayune,* 5 February 1998, sec. B, col. 1, p. 1.

Gross, Varlier. "Goshen library active in getting cards to students." *South Bend (Indiana) Tribune,* 27 August 2000, C1.

"Library campaign focuses on second-graders at Contra Costa Public Library." *San Francisco Chronicle,* 9 April 1999, A,24: 4.

"More are becoming card-carrying scholars." *Chicago Defender,* 30 November 1998, sec. C.

Pokorski, Doug. "Library cards not just for checking out books." *Springfield (Ill.) State Journal-Register,* 6 September 2000, 12.

"Signing up key players: Former NBA star helps library program recruit young users." *Los Angeles Times,* 2 July 1998, 4.

"Teens signing up for library cards can get into some shows for $5." *Pikes Peak Gazette*, 29 August 1999, LIFE6.

Vogel, Charity. "Check it out: Library's new cards to herald a new image." *Buffalo News*, 24 September 2000, C1.

WEB SITES AND WEB STORIES

For updated sites visit www.connectingya.com

"1999 library card campaign." Chicago Public Library, *http://cpl.lib.uic.edu/ 008subject/003cya/campaign98.html*.

"Austin Public Library wins two awards." Austin Public Library (June 5, 2000), *www.ci.austin.tx.us/library/06052000.htm*.

"Card campaign a success." Vigo County Public Library (Fall 2000), *http:// vax1.vigo.lib.in.us/admin/source/source.htm*.

"Celebrating success of the library's Meteor Card project: More than 1,000 kids joining the library every month." Sudbury Public Library, *www.sudbury. library.on.ca/eng/programspartners/psa/pp0449.htm*.

"Initiatives." Chicago Public Schools, *www.cps.k12.il.us/AboutCPS/Departments/Libraries/Initiatives/initiatives.html*.

LaFuente, Della. "Library's the hip place to be for card-carrying schoolkids." Chicago Sun-Times Online (November 27, 1998), *www.nabe.org/press/reprints/981127c.htm*.

"Library Card Sign-Up Month." American Library Association (September 2000), *www.ala.org/celebrating/librarycard.html*.

"Library Card Sign-Up Month news," American Library Association, *www.ala.org/pio/librarycard/librarynews.html*.

"Library Card Sign Up Month a huge success!" Rapid City Public Library (November 2000), *http://rcplib.sdln.net/NewsLetter/NewsletterFiles/00-11-Newsletter/Individual%20Articles/library_card_sign_up_month.htm*.

"Library celebrates success of card campaign." Standard Times Online (September 10, 1998), *www.texaswest.com/standard-times/news/98/october/10/ 9.htm*.

Minkel, Walter. "Five librarians, one 50-goot phone cord, and a whole lot of chutzpah." School Library Journal Online (March 1, 1999), *www.slj.com/ articles/articles/19990301_6404.asp* .

"Power Card Challenge." Houston Public Library," *www.hpl.lib.tx.us/ powercard/index.html* .

"Star Card." Austin Public Library, *www.ci.austin.tx.us/library/starcard.htm*.

INDEX

ABOUT THE AUTHOR

Patrick Jones runs Connectingya.com, a firm dedicated to consulting, training, and coaching for providing powerful youth services, including library card campaigns and Web projects. He is currently working on young adult projects in his new home of Minneapolis, as well as in California and Ohio. Jones was the youth services coordinator for the Houston Public Library in Houston, Texas, when it planned, developed, and implemented the award-winning Power Card Challenge program to register every child for a library card, and the ASPIRE after-school program for at-risk middle schoolers. ASPIRE was named by the Young Adult Library Services Association as one of the top five programs in the nation serving young adults. Jones is the author of *Connecting Young Adults and Libraries: A How-To-Do-It Manual* (Neal-Schuman, 1992). The first edition of that book was called "the classic how-to manual for the field of young adult librarianship" by *Public Libraries*. A second, revised and expanded edition was published in 1998. Jones also published in 1998 the first volume in the Scarecrow Press Young Adult series, *What's So Scary About R. L. Stine?* In April 2001 he published *Do It Right: Best Practices for Serving Young Adults in School and Public Libraries* (Neal-Schuman), written with school librarian Joel Shoemaker. In addition, Jones has written over 50 articles for such library professional publications as *Horn Book, School Library Journal, Voice of Youth Advocates*, and *Journal of Popular Culture in Libraries*, as well as essays for such reference books as *Children's Books and Their Creators, 20th Century Young Adult Authors*, and the *St. James Encyclopedia of Popular Culture*. He is a frequent speaker at library conferences across the United States, as well as in Canada, Australia, and New Zealand. He created the Web pages Young Adult Librarian's Help/Homepage and Virtual YA: A Directory of Public Library YA Web Pages. He is a former member of the board of directors of the Young Adult Library Services Association, as well as serving on the Professional Development, Quick Picks, Teen Hoopla, and Publications committee. He is cochair of the YALSA committee charged with revising the "Directions in Library Services for Young Adults" document. He is currently working on a young adult novel called *Things Change*.

I